P9-DVU-689

Rio Tinto

Lost Coconuts

Sealie Vaughn West

authorHOUSE®

AuthorHouse™
1663 Liberty Drive
Bloomington, IN 47403
www.authorhouse.com
Phone: 1-800-839-8640

© *2013 Sealie Vaughn West. All rights reserved.*

No part of this book may be reproduced, stored in a retrieval system, or transmitted by any means without the written permission of the author.

Some of the events depicted in this story are fiction. However, some of the names in this story have been changed to protect the innocent. Any similarities to the names in this story, with the exception of historical figures, places, and events, to persons or places, living or dead, are purely coincidental.

Published by AuthorHouse 10/23/2013

ISBN: 978-1-4918-2560-0 (sc)
ISBN: 978-1-4918-2561-7 (e)

Library of Congress Control Number: 2013918181

Any people depicted in stock imagery provided by Thinkstock are models, and such images are being used for illustrative purposes only. Certain stock imagery © *Thinkstock.*

This book is printed on acid-free paper.

Because of the dynamic nature of the Internet, any web addresses or links contained in this book may have changed since publication and may no longer be valid. The views expressed in this work are solely those of the author and do not necessarily reflect the views of the publisher, and the publisher hereby disclaims any responsibility for them.

Contents

ACKNOWLEDGMENTS

I have always felt that God had a hand on me, keeping me safe, even when I lived among the dangerous elements in Rio Tinto. The following passage from the Bible has been a great comfort to me:

> But those who hope in the Lord
> Will renew their strength.
> They will soar on wings like eagles;
> They will run and not grow weary,
> They will walk and not be faint.
> —Isaiah 40:31 (New International Version)

Trusting God in the face of death (all those times I should have been dead) has brought me to an assurance that God has my life in His hands.

Despite reflecting on my past, especially wanting to give up on life, living in the horrible orphanage, and battling the elements in the villages, I remained steadfast in the hope of Jesus Christ, who exchanged His life for mine. God has safely brought me from the jungles, swamps, and life-threatening circumstances of my childhood to become a citizen of the United States and to my current life, participating in the glitter of Hollywood.

I want to thank Thomas Lytle, an art teacher in Philadelphia, Pennsylvania, who mentored me as a young adult. He taught me the value of life and what it means to be a man of integrity. I'll always be grateful for his example and continued support.

My Sunday-school teacher saw a struggling Honduran child dealing with a new language. She was so patient while teaching me the Bible through sign language. She demonstrated by her example how much God loves me. Thank you.

And a final thank you to all the elders of Hope Community Church in Willow Grove, Pennsylvania. For all the support they have been to me throughout the years.

This illustration may not be used, or reproduce in any way, without the written permission of the artist. *T.L*

Lonely Grains of White Sand

Sitting on a lonely beach with nowhere to go,
watching the waves break—just to keep entertained.
Thinking of a place where I can go so I can be happy,
somewhere different from this place where I was born.
Looking at the skies, in the blue yonder a plane goes by,
looking like a comet with a long white
streak of vapor behind it.
Thinking that I could be inside this
spaceship puts a smile on my face,
knowing that it is too far away for me to reach.
All I do is wish that I could be there
someday, someday soon.

Watching the waves break, feeling
the wind hitting my face,
seeing the coconut trees sway back and forth
dancing to the rhythm of the ocean's song.
Looking at the grains of white sand, wishing
to be somewhere other than here.
Water drips down my cheek from
my eyes like a waterfall.

Just dreaming of a place where I want
to be. Not knowing where.
Asking the Maker of life to tell me—where
is this place I dream to be some day?
Just sitting with nothing to do.
Watching the waves as they sing to me, as
if I were born to be there with them.
Sitting here on a lonely beach, a million miles
from the real world that I will never know.
Never to discover what life has to offer.

I was born to hunt; I was born to fish.
Watching the fish swim on this clear sunny day,
I am more connected to them than these people.
I was born to swing a machete; I
was born to be a warrior.
On the solitary path to manhood,
in this godforsaken village
that seems to have dropped out of nowhere from the sky,
I make my own rules; I answer to no one.
I'm just nine years old, not knowing what life is all about,
Looking at the grains of white sand,
hoping that someday soon I will become a man.
I'm a warrior; I'm a hunter; I'm a
fisherman; I'm a survivor.
In this godforsaken place, I can only see the
darkness that lies before me as my destiny,
in this bleak place called Rio Tinto.

Sitting on the beach naked, just a small leaf to cover me,
watching the pretty native girls go by, thinking
that someday soon I will marry one
and take her to my house, which floats atop a coconut
tree—a small hut made of clay, with dirt floors and
the four walls made from coconut branches.
The wind blows on a lazy humid
afternoon on the white sand beach,
with my wife lying in a hammock,
under our coconut tree.
I am looking at the fluffy clouds that seem to stare back
at me, they tell me of their travels, whisper softly to me
about the places they have been and that I want to go.

I sit here on the lonely beach watching the sun go down
as the bright orange glow fades away
with each passing minute.
On top of a sand dune, looking toward
the sky to see what it tells me,
No hope in sight, just looking, counting
the white grains of sand,
and trying to pass the time, on this lonely beach,
the wind telling me that I will never
leave, no hope in sight.

So I have to get used to life as it is.
Counting grains of sand for the rest of my life
in order to keep my sanity and make sense of this.
It is my destiny. It is my life.

All I see is darkness as I sit with
tears running down my face.
I see my reflection in each wave as it breaks.
As darkness falls, it is a reminder of my desolate village.
Life, it is what it is—nothing more, nothing less.
Every day I wake up to face this
isolation, to see the same images.
I will see them for the rest of my life.
It is not an illusion; it is not a dream.
It is real; life in this village is real.

Every day I curse the Maker for a
life with no hope in sight.
I cry and I cry, as the bright orange glow fades away,
taking another minute of my life with it.
I curse Him for not having pity on the nine-year-
old boy who is sitting on this sand dune.
I wait for the bright orange glow to take me away
to the other end of the earth where another day begins.

Counting the grains of sand, on this
empty beach with no one in sight.
I have the rest of my life to count every grain one by one.
My life looks at closed doors, locked
for eternity from the world,
with no hope, just misery.
Life for me has no meaning; it is just a life.
My body is just a vessel to use to breathe;
hollow, only to carry the word "life."

The villagers make it known that "life" is just a word.
Life is cheap, our lives are nothing but grains of
sand, on a lonely beach, in a lonely place on earth,
in a lonely place to die, a place with no hope.

As another day starts, the grains of white sand
remain the same; no more, no fewer.
The same images appear before me to remind
me that life is the same every day.
This planet called Earth that appears to be
very beautiful—I live on it, I know better.
Life is not just a bad dream. Life is reality.
I have to face the sameness that appears before
me every day, whether I like it or not.
I ask myself, "What am I doing
here? How did I get here?"
The answers to these questions lie with the Maker.
He put me here for a reason I don't
understand and perhaps never will,
until I get to the end this wretched life and meet Him.

CHAPTER 1

The Pirates

Up high on Pumpkin Hill, on a hot mid-afternoon, a group of native Indian people are chopping wood for fire, clearing the bush with homemade tools. One of the men, young and strong, is wearing piercing rings all over his body—his lips, his eyelids, and one through his nose. He clears a coconut branch that is blocking his vision. The young man looks up at the sky and then toward the ocean. In the distance, he notices a dark object that is motionless on the horizon. He rubs his eyes, and then he yells to the other members of his tribe. They run towards the young man and as they approach him, he points to the object that appears to be standing still on the ocean. They are scared and all run down the hill to the village. They shout for the chief. They drag him to the water's edge, signaling and pointing.

The chief walks slowly with a slight hesitation and the rest of the men run toward the water's edge, afraid, not knowing their future with this new revelation. Talking about what it could be. There, the men try to show the chief what they saw. But the dark object is no longer in sight. The chief puts a knife to the throat of the young man for telling lies, and he threatens the others for making up stories.

The chief and the other men walk away and return to the woods and resume their work. The women are cooking food on the open flames outside of their huts. The children are playing. There's a lot of commotion going on, men trying to saddle their horses, women carrying buckets of water over their heads, children playing hide and seek. It is a normal happy day, a typical day for the kids, and for the women as they prepare the daily meals. The men are returning from hunting with the daily kill.

The young man goes back to the hilltop and watches for the dark object. After a while, he finds it again. This time, it seems bigger and clearer. He runs down the hill, yelling to the chief again. The chief is in his hut smoking a long pipe. He hears the young man yelling, but he does not pay any attention. The young man bursts into the chief's hut, out of breath and excitedly tells him what he saw again. The chief calls him a liar and threatens to kill him for being so loud and waking up the young child that had been sleeping next to him.

The young man grabs the chief by the arm and starts to drag him outside. At this time, everyone has gathered outside the chief's hut wanting to see what all the commotion is about. The chief gets out of his hut and slowly walks to the water's edge. The villagers follow at the same slow pace through the village and to the water.

The young man points to the ocean, but the object is no longer there. The chief orders some of the other men to put a rope around the young man's neck. One of the men grabs a rope and does so. As he is doing this, the object appears again on the distant horizon again. Everyone is surprised and scared, not knowing what it is. They have never seen anything like it before.

Even the chief seems scared, he orders the men to remove the rope from the young man's neck. He tells the men to prepare for war just in case. Some of the men board their canoes and row toward the object to get a closer look. Chanting native songs, the men look young and strong, as if they are ready for war. Some of them are carrying sharp homemade spears, harpoons; in one of the canoes a man stands in the front holding his spear, ready to throw it.

The men remain a safe distance while trying to explore this new floating object. They row around the vessel slowly but do not see anyone on the deck. They row around the vessel, searching curiously, looking frightened. Some of the men are standing with spears in their hands. After circling the ship several times, the men do not see anyone. They talk among themselves, telling the elder in the canoe to get closer, but the elder hesitates and tells the man in the front of the canoe to be careful.

Meanwhile, below deck the captain and his crew peer through the small windows of the ship watching the natives circle the ship.

The natives return to shore and tell the chief that they did not see anything. The natives have not seen anything from the outside world, for them to see this huge floating vessel makes them nervous, so the chief alerts all the villagers to go and take whatever they need and to go and hide. They return to their huts to secure their belongings. One of the elders gathers all the children and leads them to the woods to an underground cave they have built for protection. The children look scared as they line up to follow one of the elders to the cave. The elder grabs a torch, lights it, and shines the lighted torch around the cave illuminating the bats, snakes, spiders, spider webs, other night creatures. This is an awful place for kids. He leads them into the center of the cave. They gather in a circle, holding hands, chanting. The cave is decorated with animals' bones, human skulls, and other handmade artifacts.

The men in the village sharpen their spears and paint their faces with different colors and patterns. The chief is in his hut, smoking a pipe made from a crab claw.

The ship's captain wears a patch over his left eye, and he only has one arm. He has a scar across his face from a previous battle, so the legend goes. He waits until nightfall to send a group of his men to shore to see what is on the island. He orders his first officer to form a hunting party. The first officer gathers his men and heads for the island. They slowly and quietly row in the darkness toward the island. They scout the island quietly and return to the ship.

The next morning, a group of natives—men and women—gather near the bay. The chief puts on his huge headdress made of chicken feathers and animals' skulls, with a small human skull in the front. In the back hangs a snakeskin. He walks toward the beach to meet the ship's captain. Looking very elaborate, with their faces full of war paint, a group of elders follows him. They stare at the captain while holding sharp spears, and bows and arrows at the ready.

The natives look afraid and worried. The captain, the first officer, and a group of the men approach the shore. They get out of the dinghy, and the captain studies all of the men, women, and children. The natives look concerned, with sweat rolling down their foreheads. The captain says, "I want to talk to your leader."

The captain's men look at each other with concern, not understanding what was said.

"Who is your leader? I have a gift to give to him from Her Majesty, the queen of England." The captain laughs. He looks around, and then he turns to his men and says, "These people are dumb. They don't speak English! What language do they speak?" He turns back and looks at the natives. He walks slowly in front of them.

After many days of visiting the natives, the captain has grown to trust them, and the natives have grown to trust the captain's men. They have eaten and played together so they feel comfortable with each other now.

The captain puts his hand in his coat pocket and pulls out a mirror. All the natives are stunned at what they see—at the fact that they can see themselves. They think it is magic. They don't know what to make of it.

"See, this is for your leader. There's more where this comes from."

The chief hesitantly distances himself from the group. He looks very elaborate with his gold and silver necklace, a big feather crown on his head, and a long pipe made of gold. Not able to communicate with the stranger, he just nudges his head and points the captain to his tent. The chief orders his servants to bring something to drink and to eat.

The native servant women enter the tent while the captain and the chief are talking and laughing. The women offer the captain a wild pig's head with the eyes still in the head. The captain looks at his men and then looks away, closing his eyes in disgust. The women stand in front of him, still offering him the food. The chief is watching with a smile on his face. The chief and his men take pieces of the smoked meat and eat it. The captain looks around at the other men eating, so he grabs some of the meat from the pig's head and eats too.

The captain says, "Men! We'd better eat. We do not want to insult these bastards and have us be their next meal."

The captain very reluctantly picks up a gold cup and raises it to his lips. He asks, "What is this?" He notices that it's red. "It looks like blood!" The rest of the men stop and look at the captain. The captain takes a drink and spits it out. "This shit tastes like rotten blood!" His men laugh.

The captain and the other men are eating and drinking like wild savages and are playing with the women, touching and kissing them.

The chief brings out a chest and he orders one of the natives to open it. The captain is amazed at the gold and silver he sees. Later, he comes out of the tent and calls his men to head back to the ship. The chief and the other natives walk with the captain to the water's edge, singing native songs, dancing, and laughing.

The captain looks back at the natives who are waving and laughing.

Later that night, the captain calls his first officer. "I want you to form a party and go to the island. Kill all of these bastards."

The young lieutenant looks at the captain with amazement. "Sir," says the lieutenant, "You mean kill them all, sir?"

The captain, smoking his pipe, sits down in a chair made out of animals' bones. "That is exactly what I mean. I want their gold and silver."

The lieutenant, still looking amazed, says, "Sir, you want me to do this tonight?" The captain feeds his bird. "Yes, lieutenant, tonight, before sunup."

The lieutenant goes below deck to the sleeping quarters and looks around at the men, he says, "The captain wants me to go ashore and get rid of 'em."

The men look at each other with amazement.

"So I'm going with twelve of you."

They all try to volunteer. One of the men says, "I'm going to take some of them women and bring them here so they can serve me, every night!"

"Enough," says the lieutenant. "Let's get ready. We only have a few hours left until sun-up."

The captain is in his quarters looking into the dark night, staring at the island. He's smoking his pipe with his bird on his shoulder. He sees his lieutenant boarding the dinghy with the twelve men.

The captain goes on deck and shouts, "I want all men on deck and to the battle stations, at once."

All of the men run from their bunks onto the deck. At their battle stations, they aim their cannons at the island.

The captain orders, "Men, on my command, I want to fire at them bastards, and aim good."

The lieutenant approaches the island very quietly, and the men surround the villager's huts and set them on fire. The native men, women, and children run terrified, screaming. The men fight with spears. There is total chaos. The lieutenant with his coat covered in blood, one of his legs with an open wound, lays helpless with a villager's body on top of him. One of his men comes and removes the body rolling it to the side.

Meanwhile, on the ship, the captain orders all stations to stand by, to be ready to fire on his command. "Once we get the signal from the lieutenant."

As the sun rises, the captain leans against the superstructure on the starboard side of the ship, smoking his pipe with satisfaction. He stares, emotionless, at the smoky island. He boards one of his dinghies with the rest of his men following who cheer at the prospect of killing.

They get to the shore, and can barely see through the smoke that is enveloping the island. The captain, walking slowly, looks around and stumbles upon a young villager's body. He spits on it. As he surveys the devastation he has brought to these people, he hears a familiar voice and enters a smoky hut, and he sees his young lieutenant with blood running down his jacket and a spear in his chest. The captain calls the other men.

The young lieutenant lies helpless, looking at the captain, tears rolling down his bloody face, and he says, "I failed you! Papa, I failed you."

The captain looking down at him sadly says, "A job done well, my son! A bloody job done well, my son!" The men surround their fallen comrade, sadness showing on their faces. The captain orders the men to sort through the rest of the bodies and separate them, the women in one pile and the men in another, the children all together. The men gathered all the bodies and pile them accordingly as the captain ordered.

The captain grabs the spear that is in the young lieutenant's chest and looks at him.

"My son!" says the captain.

He pulls the spear out. The lieutenant screams. The captain kneels down and puts his son's head in his lap. The lieutenant looks at the captain with tears rolling down his cheeks as if to say something, but he just closes his eyes and takes his last breath. The captain sobbing holds his son's head on his arms.

The captain orders the men to dig a hole nearby. The men carry the lieutenant's body and gently put his body in the hole. The captain says, with tears rolling down his face, "Men, this is my son! My son gave his life! Just as God who, gave his son! I do not feel any remorse for the fact that my son is going to hell."

With the smoke from the attack lingering in the air around the island, the men cover the grave of the young lieutenant. The captain waits at the water's edge, looking at the horizon, feeling proud of the battle, but sad for the loss of his son. He orders the rest of the men to put the bodies at the other side of the island and to gather all of the gold and silver to be brought back to the ship.

The smoky, lonely island lies quietly with no sound to be heard for miles. There is only smoke and bodies—of men, women, and children—and lots of blood.

The rest of the captain's men have tears in their eyes grieving for the loss of their close brother and shipmate—some of them are wounded, others are bloody. The calm breeze blows, and the smoke of death and the smell of blood hang in the air. The island that once existed peacefully with the laughter and noise of children playing fades into the abyss of forgotten civilization.

CHAPTER 2

Luther

Ten years later . . . an old bearded man in his well-worn and dirty clothes, who is in his early fifties and has most of his front teeth missing, is on a small tattered single-sail ship and floats somewhere in the Atlantic Ocean. With a light wind, there is only the sound of the ocean slapping against the vessel. In the hot mid-day sun, the man leans on the tiller and squints as he looks up at the clear sky. He watches a bird flying overhead. He surveys the direction of the wind with one finger. He reaches for his weathered jug of whiskey and pours it into an old mason jar. While taking a sip, he makes a face, drinks more, and then continues smoking the small stub of a cigar.

He's enjoying the day, the stillness of the ocean, cruising with the light wind. He stomps his foot on the deck. Talking to himself and to the people down below, he shouts, stomps his foot again, and sips from the jar again.

"You dumb animals, better bring me good money."

Coughing hard and spitting on the deck, he leans over the side and extends his arms to touch the water.

"I'm getting tired of this damn shit. Yes, sir!"

Holding his jar in a toast, he slurs, "This drink is in the name of the damn queen! All you dumb animals down below who don't like me swearing the name of the queen, damn you, too. After being on the sea for as long as I have, first I see a dumb bird that has been following me, now I don't know what I see! Men tend to see things they do not want to see even if it is land, land, land. You hear me, animals? I see land! Land! In the name of the bloody queen of bloody England, I see land! Now I will sell you all and make gold. It has to be an English land. What if it is not? We are all going to be dead!"

Luther's vessel approaches the land and drops anchor. He sticks his head below deck and shouts over the loud cry of a child, "I'm going to go ashore. All you bitch animals better behave. You're all going to bring me lots of money."

He gets into his dinghy and heads toward shore. Astor Hill, a slim white Englishman in his early forties, stands at the water's edge with a paper and a pen in his hands watching the approaching dinghy.

Luther docks, gets out of the dinghy and introduces himself. "Sir, my name is Luther Lowell, from Her Majesty the bloody queen of England, at your service."

The Englishman replies, "Well, from the bloody queen of England, I'm Astor Hill, at your service sir, and what might you be carrying in your vessel? More Negro slaves?"

Luther responds rather cautiously, "Well sir, Mr. Hill, would you be interested in trading some of my Negro slaves for some British pounds or, perhaps a meal and a bath? All of my Negro slaves are strong and can offer you much."

Astor Hill looks rather interested, and smiles, "I have property here on the island and I already have a few Negro slaves, perhaps not as strong as yours, sir. Luther, perhaps we can talk later, but there is a man named Henry Morgan on this island who would be much interested in your Negroes. I will go to his house tonight, and I will mention to him that you have Negro slaves and that you are looking to trade for gold."

"Yes! Yes!" Luther exclaims while scratching his head and then under his armpits. "I need a bath and a shave. I have not taken a bath in months," he says looking rather disturbed. "Well, I'll be at the saloon. I need a drink, lots of drinks. Being at sea for as long as I have, a man loses his spirits and needs to recharge."

Luther approaches the Bucket of Blood saloon. He enters and orders a drink.

The bartender, a fellow British man in his sixties with a half-beard and a cigar in his mouth, looks at Luther and says, "You, sir, are not from these islands. I have never seen anyone quite like you around these parts."

Luther looks at him with one eye, holding the drink close to his mouth, "That is because I'm not from these parts. I come from the Cayman Islands. Do you know where that is, sir? And I have cargo on my ship and a little one, too. His name is Pita. His Negro mama has given birth to him on my vessel. Can you believe that? So I'm going to name him Pita."

The bartender looks at him and says, "Why Pita? Sounds like an animal name. I have a dog and his name is Queen. Hail to the queen."

Luther returns to his vessel. He goes below deck, grabs a lantern, and looks at the slaves one by one. He stops at the baby sleeping in his mother's arms. The other slaves are watching. Luther grabs an old bucket, flips is over and sits on it. He shines the lantern on the mother and child. He reaches into his pocket for some tobacco and wipes his mouth.

"I've been thinking, you both can earn me lots of money, gold, but I think that I will not sell you."

Looking at the boy, Luther says to the slave woman, "I have named him Pita. I do not know what it means, but I like it."

The woman looks rather scared and is sweating. She has tears rolling down her face.

Luther stands up, kicks the bucket away and starts to head back to the deck. He stops and surveys his cargo one more time with a smile in his face. "I have heard about a man who may be interested in the rest of you savages. If all goes as planned, tomorrow I will get rid of all of you, except for her and the child. They stay. She will raise him and he will serve *me*. You all are going to remember my name. I have burned my name on each one of you. Tomorrow, the child is going to be branded just like the rest!

Luther, with a whip in his hand, grabs one of the Negro men, rips off his shirt, and turns him around to show his initials—L.L. The Negro drops to the ground, landing with his face in the hay. The rest of the slaves can only look on. Below deck it is unbearably hot, all of the slaves are wet with sweat and frightened of the prospect of what is to happen to them. The mothers are holding their children tight to their bodies.

The next day, Luther returns to the saloon. He orders a drink, and asks the bartender if he knows a man by the name of Henry Morgan. "I understand he has lots of property on the island."

A man who is in his fifties, a rather good-looking businessman with white hair, approaches the bar and asks for a drink. He has a whip in his hand and is wearing a pair of knee-high boots. He looks Luther up and down noticing his dirty shirt and overall unclean appearance.

"You sir," the man says, "and who might you be, asking for me? I have never laid eyes on you in my life and you're asking for me? What type of business do you want with me?"

"Sir, I beg your pardon. My name is Luther Lowell from Her Majesty the queen of England. I come to sell you the savage Negroes I have on my vessel. I understand you have property and you might be interested in them. I have a dozen strong, energetic Negroes, and I'm willing to make a deal with you."

Henry looks rather skeptical. "Are you an Englishman? What part of the islands do you happen to drop from, sir?"

Luther sips his drink, "I have come a long way with my Negroes. All the way from the Cayman Islands."

They leave the bar together and walk toward the dock. Henry finally says, "Go and get your Negroes and let me see what you have before I change my mind and kick you off my island."

Luther returns to the vessel and brings the slaves to the deck one by one and lines them up. He puts the shackles on each one of them and connects the shackles with a heavy chain. He lines up the men near the edge of the boat and looks at them.

"All you animals stink like dogs." Luther turns the male slave on the end around to face the water and, with his foot, pushes him over the side. The slaves are pulled along with him and drop into the water after him. "You all need a bath, pigs," laughs Luther.

The men in the water try to stay afloat, try to swim. Luther boards his dinghy and grabs one of the slaves and pulls him up into the boat and leaves the rest struggling to stay afloat in the water.

As they approach the dock, Henry, still holding his whip in hand, is rather surprised by Luther's behavior.

Luther tows the slaves to shore. The man at the far end of the chain is going under and no longer struggling, so Luther grabs his arms and drags him out of the water. Luther turns the man onto his back and steps on his chest, pushing with his foot. "Live, you dog! Live! You are my property. You cannot die on me yet. I own you, you cannot die on me!" After a few hard thrusts, the man comes around and spits out the water that had filled his lungs.

Luther walks all the slaves to the center of town. Some of the slaves are struggling to walk, trying to catch their breath. They are then displayed in an open courtyard. He entices Henry to buy them all by telling him how strong they are, touching the men's muscles and showing him their strong necks.

Luther boasts, "I've got a young one and his mother on the ship, but they are not for sale, just these strong dogs. These Negroes will bring you lots of wealth and work your property."

Henry with a smile in his face replies, "How do you know they will not run away?"

Luther turns and says, "Well, Mr. Morgan, if they run, kill 'em. You can do that, can't you? Very simple."

Henry walks toward the slaves. He inspects them very closely, and then he turns one of them around to see his back. He notices the initials *L.L.*

"These markings, Luther. I have to put my own initials on each one of them now," says Henry. "Luther, you are a terrible Englishman, but you have a deal. I will buy your pigs. Now they are my pigs." Henry cracks his whip, and the slaves jump. "Luther, come back tomorrow, and I will have your dirty pounds. And, bring me the young one. I want to see him."

"No!" says Luther. "He and the mother are not for sale. They are mine, and I will keep them, and I will do as I please. Thank you, sir."

Luther returns to his ship and goes to the woman. "I have sold all of your kind." Luther makes a small fire in a bucket and opens a small sack that he has under his coat.

He brings it out and shows it to her. It's the branding iron with the initials *L.L.*

"He is ready, just like you were ready." Luther sticks the rod in the fire. "Prepare the child for me, woman. Bring him to me, and move away before I kill you and you'll not see your child become what I make him."

When the iron is hot enough and glowing red, Luther grabs the child by the arm. The mother is crying and being difficult. Luther lays the child across his lap, grabs the blistering rod and aims it the boy's back.

Now back at home in the Cayman Islands, Luther enters his favorite smoky saloon with a few of his crew. They sit at a table talking about the day's events, their experiences while they were in England, and how they are going to make more money by selling slaves. Luther says, "Men, I found this island not too far from here, and I like the island. It is called Utila. It's very small, and I think I will move there soon with my family."

The men who are smoking cigars and chewing tobacco look at him and at each other and start laughing. One of the men looks at Luther and says, "Luther you are crazy! You're not leaving the Cayman Islands, are you?"

Luther, with his drink in hand, looks at the man and says, "I'm tired of sailing all over with my slaves. One of these times, they're all going to die on me. I need to care for my family. My son Ernest is getting to be a big boy. I need to show him new things."

Luther stands up from the table and starts walking toward the door of the saloon. He stumbles on his way out and falls flat on his face. A man yells, "There goes an Englishman, flat on his bloody face like the queen." Everybody in the saloon laughs. They lift their glasses and make a toast to the Englishman and the queen. The men yell, "Hail the queen!"

Luther gets up, brushes himself off and leaves. He stumbles toward his house. He opens the front door, he sees his wife Viola. He tries to say something and falls to the floor. Viola is very petite, simple, and conservative British woman. She's a rather attractive middle-aged English woman. "You stupid fool!" she says. She grabs both of his arms and drags him to the hammock. She pulls a small chair near and starts to hum "Amazing Grace." Viola is very loyal to Luther, she doesn't understand him much, but she tries to support him in his endeavors. She is tired of Luther's demands and weary of taking care of her drunken husband.

Viola lights a candle, strips off his worn boots, pours some fresh water from a kettle, washes his feet, and prepares him for bed.

The next morning, Luther walks toward the beach limping from an old injury, wearing no shirt. He starts to clean and do repairs in his new and bigger rig. Luther and Viola do not get along very well these days. They frequently fight, but sometimes they drink together and talk about their home country, Britain, and how they first met at the dock one afternoon when Luther came back from days away out to sea. Viola was buying fish. Luther approached her to offer a slave to cook for her. This was his way of flirting.

After a few months of seeing each other, Viola invited him to meet her parents. They were married and Luther took her away on his fifty-foot sail boat, never to return to England.

These days, Luther is very violent toward Viola. When he is drunk, which is often, he curses at her and beats her for no reason. If his food is cold or his fish is not prepared the way he likes it, or if the dumplings he has to have at every meal are not properly baked, or worse, not served at all, he beats her up. They have been married for many years. Her life with him has been difficult. She used to be quite an attractive woman but now, her hair is gray and most of her teeth are missing or half rotten. Despite Luther's shortcomings as a husband, she supports him and does not leave him.

One evening, while eating dinner with his wife and his son, Ernest, Luther says, "We are moving to the island of Utila. There we can make a real home and live with British families. Tomorrow we start packing and will leave when we are ready. We are going to take all of our slaves and all of our belongings."

Viola looks at him in amazement. "You old fool. You're moving and taking all of your Negro slaves? Why don't you feed them to the sharks? You just cannot live without them, can you?"

Ernest jumps out his chair and eagerly heads to get the sailboat ready so they can leave for Utila. That evening, Ernest excitedly goes all over the neighborhood telling the neighbors he and the family are moving to Utila.

"So what do you do with the coconuts?" asks Luther.

"I take them to the States," says Henry. "There are a lot of possibilities, the American's are eager to buy coconuts from us. Maybe you should move to the coast and raise coconuts. There's a place south of Tela called Rio Tinto where the land is rich and full of palms with coconuts. You need to go and see it."

The next day, Luther boards his boat and heads toward the coast of Honduras to a place called Rio Tinto where the coconut palms flourish. It is a very isolated place.

After seeing the village and all of its potential, he travels back to the Cayman Islands and buys dozens of slaves. He loads them on his ship and travels with them to Rio Tinto. As the villagers see a boat approaching, they all run to the water's edge and start singing. The native men board their small canoes and row toward the boat.

Luther drops anchor a distance from the shore. He stands on the deck of the boat and watches the villagers on the shore chanting and waving while some of the men approach the boat.

Luther goes below and, minutes later, comes out with a string of slaves in chains. The men and woman wear shackles on their necks and ankles. Some of them are bleeding and some are in bad health. He lines them up on the deck.

Luther stands on the deck of the boat, looking very confident facing the shore. He yells, "My children" "My children, you are all my children, I brought you from hell, I'm your master. I have returned again from a long voyage. Now I bring you the rest of your brothers and sisters whom you have not seen for a long time."

He pulls a machete from the holster he carries under his arm. He waves the machete at the slaves. Luther's boat is surrounded with villagers waiving palms, happy to see him, eager to hear him. "Again, I'm your master. If you ever betray me, there are going to be consequences. You will deal with me!" I'm Luther your master, don't you ever forget that, if you ever run from me I will hunt you with my dogs and I will let the dogs eat you alive, you remember that." He turns, walks toward the slaves, and looks from one to the next into their eyes.

They tremble with fear, sweat drips down their faces. Luther signals for them to stand near the edge of the boat. They gradually move, barely able to walk from the pain of the shackles rubbing against their skin.

"All you animals stink like pigs. You're all going to take a bath." He moves behind of one of them, lifts his left foot and kicks him overboard into the water. They are all dragged in after him, one by one they go overboard into the water, screaming.

The villagers in the boats rush to rescue the slaves. Laughing, looking at them trying to stay afloat, Luther says, "That is one way to get you off my boat, you savages!"

Later that night, it is very dark. The stars are so bright and so close. It is so dark you can almost touch the darkness. All the villagers build a huge bonfire in the middle of the small village. They are dancing, singing, and drinking. They seem to be having a great time. Luther, sitting on the sidelines with a whip over one shoulder, sips a cup of moonshine with lime watching the dancers and everybody celebrating. He gets up and walks around in the crowd, smiling and hugging some of the women and kissing them on their cheeks.

Luther orders one of his slaves to get his horse. The middle-aged slave brings him his beautiful white dappled horse. Luther mounts the horse and heads toward the ocean. He rides on the beach enjoying the day, smoking a cigar—taking a short break from the immense responsibilities of running his coconut empire.

He returns home and then through his property to observe the workers. He dismounts and gives the horse to a slave. He walks to where the workers are peeling coconuts then over to where others are chopping coconuts in half and putting them in a wooden tent. These tents are made of bamboo, about ten feet long, three feet high with bamboo slots in the middle, to lay the coconut on top. They are making copra. To make copra, you cut the coconuts in half and roast them on an open fire or leave them out in the hot sun. When they cool, the resulting brown chunks have a sweet taste.

Men and woman are working in the hot sun. Luther has a cup of water in his hand. The workers are sweating. He goes and lies in his hammock under a coconut tree enjoy the softly blowing breeze and the empire he is building. Luther is very flamboyant and full of life. He is now in his mid-fifties with graying hair. He has nothing to worry about. His wife, Viola, is back on the island, of Utila. He's all by himself except for the slaves working the coconut plantation.

He has nearly fifteen hundred acres of coconut trees capable of producing a million coconuts a month. He has a huge warehouse made of lumber, some additional smaller that look like huts. All of this is near his house. He also has accumulated a large amount cows, pigs, chickens, horses, and more slaves to pick coconuts. Young and old, men and women, all can be seen in the hot sun picking coconuts. The only way for him to communicate with his slaves is through gestures; very few of them understand English.

When ships come to buy Luther's coconuts, Luther makes a big production of the event. He dresses in his finest clothes. Slaves wait outside of his house while gets dressed. When he is ready, he struts out smoking a cigar, to the bamboo chair he has had made for his transport to meet with the captains of the ships. A few of his strongest slaves carry him like a king to the water's edge in the comfort of his bamboo chair.

One captain of a particular ship is a very rugged, strong, middle-aged Englishman. He looks as if his skin is burned—either that or he's had too much English liquor. His face looks like dried leather. His name is Foster Cooper.

As usual on this, his monthly visit to Rio Tinto, Foster comes to shore in his dinghy carrying a strong rustic briefcase. The price of coconuts is very high on the market so Luther stands in front of his slaves with a huge smile on his face. Foster gets out of his dinghy. He and Luther exchange handshakes and greetings. Luther invites him for tea. Both men are carried in Luther's throne back to the house.

They sit on the porch, smoking cigars. "So, how many coconuts do you have for me this month?" Foster asks Luther.

"This has been a very good month for me," says Luther. "I have one hundred and fifty good slaves working for me so I take advantage of them." Luther swings a flyswatter with his right hand and is smoking a cigar with his left. Foster gives Luther the case. Luther opens it and he sees nothing but American dollars.

"Twenty-five thousand gold American dollars," says Foster. He can't help but notice Luther's face light up in when he sees that all of that green gold. They call the dollar "gold" on the islands.

Luther orders his slaves to take the coconuts to the shoreline and load Foster's boat. Luther walks with Foster toward his warehouses and shows him the coconuts he has harvested. All of slaves are making the preparations to take the coconuts out of the warehouses to the waiting ship.

"You've been busy," says Foster.

"I have been more than busy, my dear bother," says Luther. Both men walk around the warehouses, Luther smoking a long pipe and Foster smoking a long cigar.

The workers are filling sacks of coconuts, counting them one by one. Some are lifting sacks of heavy coconuts on their shoulders. At the shoreline, some are loading the coconuts into canoes and taking them to the ship. Sweat pours down their foreheads and their faces reflect their exhaustion. It appears to be a well-orchestrated operation with so many workers scurrying about they look like ants in a colony.

While the women are making cassava, Luther walks around with a whip on his shoulder, overseeing all of the men working. He's sucking his long pipe and smiling.

After almost ten hours of watching the hard slave labor, Foster thanks Luther for his hospitality and for the smoke. Luther, his ego and his wallet satisfied, thanks him also. Foster boards his small dinghy and heads back to his ship. With the sun setting on the horizon, Luther leans back in one of his canoes and watches as the ship sets sail—remembering when he, too, went sailing to far-off lands.

It's a hot summer night. There's a bonfire at the side of the house and some of the workers, slaves and natives are gathered around it. They're singing native songs and playing native drums. Luther is lying in a hammock on his porch, smoking his pipe, and thoroughly enjoying what he has accomplished. Luther whispers to one of his servants to go and get one of the young girls who is dancing and bring her to him.

The servant approaches the young girl and whispers in her ear. She looks surprised. She shakes her head to say no, so grabs her arm and forces her toward the porch. She doesn't really have a choice. The others stop and watch as she dragged away.

The young girl sits next to Luther with her head down. Luther shines a lantern on her face, smiles and sends her to get cleaned up and then to Luther's bedroom.

When she arrives, he is lying face down on his bed with only sheet covering his buttocks. The young girl stands next to the bed, looking down, frightened. Luther turns to look at her and orders her to massage him with oil. She reluctantly puts her hands on his shoulders. Hesitating, she massages him. Luther lies there, enjoying the feel as she presses her hands into his body.

He turns over to look at her and holds her hand. The young girl is surprised and is breathing hard. She looks at him. He reaches to her and touches her face; slowly sliding his hand down he loosens her dress. It drops to the ground. He looks at her naked body. The young woman closes her eyes. He forces her to lie down next to him. With tears rolling down her cheeks, she begs him to let her go. He says, "I will teach you a few things about the English people and life."

The next day, around midmorning, the whole village gathers at the river for the ceremonial ritual. The native Garifuna people of Rio Tinto have a coming-of-age celebration for the male children.

All of the elders watch from the water's edge while the fathers are gathered in a large circle in their canoes in the river; their sons sit with them in the canoes. Women are chanting on the shore holding palm branches. A couple of strong men are on the other side of the river holding onto a large crocodile. They have tied a rope around the mouth of this huge animal. It jumps and thrashes while the men try to keep the animal still. One of the men in the canoe picks up a child who is around five or six years old. He lifts the child into the air to bless him. The women's singing gets louder and louder as the man holds the child in the air.

One of the elders, standing at the riverbank, calls to the men to let the dedication begin. The women keep chanting. Everybody keeps waving the palm branches. Some of the women are dancing, calling for the gods to bless their children. The man holding the child brings him to the shore. The crocodile continues to struggle and the men try to keep the crocodile down. They place the boy on crocodile and tie him to its back. They tie the boy down tight, the boy is crying hysterically. The noise from the women's chanting grows louder. They're chanting songs that ask the gods to bless their boys so they will survive this and grow up to be strong men.

The crocodile is thrashing and jumping with the boy is tied to the back. The men drag the crocodile into the water by the rope tied around its neck. The crocodile dives underwater. The men pull on the rope. The crocodile, resisting, comes up. The boy is still on the back of the animal! The women are dancing, chanting, and waving palm branches. The crocodile plunges back underwater.

After only a few seconds that seem like an eternity the men pull the crocodile back up. The boy is still tied to the crocodile, but now he's on the belly of the crocodile. The boy has survived the traditional test of being a strong man. The men untie the child, clean him up, and take him to the elders and present him as a strong man. They hold the boy in the air and present him to his mother. The ritual then continues with the next child.

Some boys make it and others don't. Some come up with no arms or legs. They are the ones who are not worthy. The celebration starts early in the morning. It lasts all day. Every boy has to go through this test of manhood.

Luther mounts his horse and rides to survey his cattle. He rides along surveying all of the male slaves working to tend the cattle. He gestures to one of the slaves that one of the calves is out of the corral. He rides to the river, dismounts and stands at the riverbank for some time. He takes off his clothes and jumps in. He notices an attractive slave Negro woman approaching the river to get water. Luther gets out of the water naked and extends his hand to her. When she sees him, she screams, and tries to run. He catches her from behind and takes her into the water with him. He holds her tight as she struggles, kissing her and forcing himself inside her. These slaves work for Luther; he thinks that they ought to do whatever he asks. He owns them.

Later that evening, the natives gather around a bonfire. The men play the drums and sing. Luther sits on the porch of his small hut, which is built on stilts made from coconut trunks. He lives a very modest life despite the wealth he has accumulated.

He watches the celebration and gets drunk on moonshine. He mounts his horse and rides to the center of the ceremonies. He charges toward the door of one of the huts. The horse hesitates and rears up, but Luther kicks hard with his spurs and forces him into the hut. There are a few women around the clay stove cooking within the hut. Still on horseback, Luther's inside the house. He picks up one of the Negro slave women and takes her with him into the dark woods.

Luther likes to take advantage of his slaves and use them. He especially likes to use the women for his own personal pleasures, and he does not care much about their well-being. He makes them live in the worst condition possible, but he always makes sure that they serve him well sexually.

Luther has been very prosperous with his coconut plantation, he has made lots of money, and he has lots of cattle that he sells to other merchants. He is a very savvy businessman with no heart and feeling for anyone.

Although Luther has lots of money, he does not know what to do with it, so he hides it. Only he knows where he hides it. He has money stashed in burlap sacks in the attic of his house and buried throughout the property. Every time Foster comes to buy coconuts, he hands Luther a burlap sack full of money. The money is not in pesos; it's in U.S. dollars—large bills, all in burlap sacks.

Luther smokes from a pipe of mahogany made especially for him by one of the slaves. As he sits on his porch, he pulls a one-hundred-dollar bill from his pocket and lights it, just to see it burn. He lights his pipe and then holds it and watches it until it burns his fingers. Sometimes he makes a bonfire with sacks full of money and dances around the fire, celebrating the burning of money. He says, "It's just damn money." He laughs like a crazy man as the smoke envelops him from his expensive fire.

After twenty years, now in his mid-sixties, living in the small village of Rio Tinto with the slaves he brought with him from the Cayman Islands, Luther has become very difficult. He is even more aggressive than he used to be, but still confident about what he needs to accomplish. He goes to great lengths just to prove himself a competent businessman. He's very flamboyant, and he loves the women.

Luther has built an empire for himself in Rio Tinto with the coconut plantation. He has almost three thousand acres of coconuts now. He has two hundred and fifty. The ones who betray him, he shoots on the spot. He has publicly executed more than a few who have tried to escape.

He brings the ones he catches to the front of his house and holds a public tribunal to show the others what will happen if anyone else has any ideas about running away or betraying him. He has them tied with a heavy rope; puts shackles on their ankles, hands, and neck; and chains them to a coconut tree. There he gathers the rest of the slaves and they are made to play drums for the special occasion of public humiliation and execution. The slaves are executed either by being dragged into the ocean to become shark bait, or by being hanged, or by being turned loose in the woods to be chased by the dogs until they are caught then shot by Luther. This is a sport to him, a celebration of power—something for him to do with his spare time.

He has created a world of his own. No one can penetrate his world. Visitors from the island of Utila will come and visit him to see how he's doing, and he treats them like royalty. He offers the men companionship by giving them some of the young slave girls from the village. This goes on often. The men who know him well come and visit regularly.

Luther lived to be an old man, he was always very aware of his surroundings and kept track of his slaves. No one in the family remembers how he died or where he died. Some say that he went back to the island of Utila to be with his family. Some say he was killed by the villagers and they put his body somewhere in the jungle. Some say he rode his horse into the ocean and drowned. However he died, surely it was very elegant and very dramatic. He was a dramatic man, a cold man, with no affection, living only to satisfy his own ego.

I imagine Luther, my great-grandfather, riding like the wind on horseback along the beach, shirtless with his arms spread out wide, into the sunset until he can go no farther. Jumping with his horse into the Atlantic Ocean, saying, "Till death do us part damned queen!" There he meets his Maker and answers for all the bad he did in his life.

I also imagine, that all the people he left behind, like his slaves, his wife, and his son, Ernest (my grandfather) might be rejoicing over his death.

Chapter 3

Ernest Lowell

Ernest is the only son of Luther and Viola Lowell. Now, he is in his early forties. He has lived on the island of Utila most of his life. He speaks no Spanish. Both of his parents are British. He and his wife, Prudence, have three children: Carmela, Sealie, and Ernest. Since they do not use "junior" in Honduras, the young Ernest is just Ernest, but his mother nicknames him "Kusa."

Prudence is a very simple and modest woman who always wears solid-color dresses. She has graying hair, but is still very attractive although she never wears any makeup. She's pleasant, but she does not talk much. She is always by her husband's. She is either cooking or crocheting. She loves to mend Ernest's pants and make her own clothes.

World War II has ended, and the price of coconuts is very high. It varies from seven cents to twenty cents per coconut. That is very expensive. All of the coconuts sold in Rio Tinto are being delivered to the States, Belize, the Cayman Islands, the Bahamas—all of these islands are very prosperous because of coconuts, but not like Rio Tinto. Ernest is carrying on the legacy of his father by continuing to build an empire from coconut plantations. He has constructed three huge sheds the size of football fields capable of holding more than a million coconuts. He has stored almost a half million coconuts and almost fifty tons of copra in sacks in all of the sheds. Ernest negotiates according to the highest price in the market. He is a very shrewd businessman. He was taught well by his father.

He is also a very selfish man, with no feelings toward anyone. Money along with the power of having a very hot commodity drives him. He has also learned these traits from his father.

By the time Ernest comes to Rio Tinto, after living on Utila Bay Island, after his father's death, the slaves are free people and the population is growing. The native Garifuna live side-by-side with the free slaves. These slaves are very loyal to the Lowell family. Ernest and Prudence have four maids working for them at the house, and fifty or more men on the plantation. These people are not being paid much. Ernest does not like them because of their color of skin, and he pushes them very hard for that reason.

His wife, Prudence, is more kind toward them. She looks after their children when they are sick and looks after the men while they are working. Ernest is totally against what Prudence is doing.

Prudence goes out of her way to see that the village children are in good health by going to their homes and visiting, talking to them, checking their pulses, and cleaning the wounds caused by machetes. Four strong men carry her in a chair through the village when she goes to look after the families.

The villagers love her. Every time she comes to a hut, they bow down to her and give her hugs and kisses on the cheek. She is modest and doesn't pay too much attention to all of the affection that they show toward her. She sees a child unable to walk because he has a bad machete wound that is full of worms, and she orders the men to carry the child to her house. This is Luther and Viola's that was handed down. She takes the child into her home and cares for her until the little one becomes well.

While Prudence carries on her philanthropic work, Ernest is occupied with his plantation—running up and down on his horse, making sure that the men are working and the cattle are taken care of.

Luther left Ernest the whole plantation of coconut palms. He inherited the plantation and about two hundred head of cattle. He took over the plantation with his two grown sons, Sealie and Kusa (young Ernest) and his daughter, Carmela.

Ernest is a busy man. He hardly has any time to spend with his family. He stays up all night making copra. Copra is used as cooking and body oil. It is sold on the open market to supplement the income from the coconuts alone. Ernest has the workers build tent-shaped structures that look like railroad trestles. They are about four-feet high and fifteen to twenty-feet long with spacers between the bamboo culms. The coconuts are cut in half and put on top of the bamboo structures with the meat facing down.

A fire is built on the ground inside the structure so that the flames barely touch the coconut. He has men working making copra twenty-four hours a day, tons of it. And, all the whole coconuts that they produce in a day are put in huge long sheds. They are stored in these sheds until someone comes and buy them.

Juney Cooper is a rough-looking, short Englishman from the island of Utila. He is the son of Foster Cooper. Juney lives in Utila. He travels from village to village buying coconuts. Once a month, Juney comes and buys coconuts and copra from Ernest Lowell. That is always a very special day because people from other parts of the world in Rio Tinto are rarely seen. So when Juney comes, it's a celebration. All the plantation workers are happy. Ernest has them carry the coconuts to the beach and from there they load the coconuts in canoes and take them to Juney's boat. It is a massive production line. Some of the women cook for the men. Others stand in line with buckets of water for the men who are working in the hot sun. They sing native songs or just something they made up. They support their loved ones.

Ernest and Juney oversee the loading of the coconuts and copra. Both men, smoking cigars, seems to be enjoying the whole affair. Ernest tells Juney how he hates the colored workers, but he likes how they work. Juney tells him about what is happening on the island of Utila and to the family he still has there.

The work goes on all day, nonstop. The men work without stopping until the end of the day or until every last coconut is out of the sheds. After it is all over, Juney goes back to his boat, picks up a metal case, and brings it back to Ernest. With a big smile on his face, Ernest opens the case, he looks inside and pulls out the large sack of American dollars; fifty thousand dollars in American "gold." He shakes hands with Juney, puts the sack over his shoulders, and walks home.

One time, Ernest makes a trip to Utila in Juney's boat. He goes to see an old friend of his, Astor Hill, a typical Englishman. He is just like the rest of them, always in the saloons, drinking whiskey, and talking gossip about everyone in town. He keeps up with all the news hearsay on the island of Utila.

They talk for a while, and Ernest asks Astor to make him a thirty-foot sailboat. So Astor does just that. After some time when the boat is completed, Ernest makes another trip to Utila to pick up his boat and sets sail back to Rio Tinto. Talk abound an awesome boat! It is the most beautiful thing on the ocean. He names it *Hikity*. I have no idea what the name means, but with its two immense sails, it's just fantastic!

By this time, Ernest is making lots of money. Every time Juney comes, he brings Ernest a sack full of money. Juney makes this trip to buy coconuts either every month or every other month. Ernest does not know what to do with all of his wealth. He is hiding the sacks under the house, digging holes under the foundation without anyone knowing it. Not even Prudence knows how much money they have.

On more than one or two occasions, Ernest sets sail in his thirty-foot sailboat with a crew of ten and seventy thousand dollars and goes to the city of Puerto Cortes. He says that he's going to buy merchandise. He stays away for a week or so, spending money on liquor and giving money away to the women he meets.

Lighting cigarettes with hundred-dollar bills and throwing money into the sea is not a big deal to him. The other men just look on in disbelief as he throws money into the ocean. Ernest gets so drunk, he can't even steer the boat on his way home, but he will not let anyone else steer! Upon his return, Prudence is always waiting for him. She watches him try to come ashore. He isn't even able to get into the dinghy to get to the shore. So he just falls overboard and tries to swim ashore.

All the times he goes to the city and spends money on women and partying in the bars, and lighting cigarettes with dollar bills, never, ever does he buy anything for Prudence; not even a dress or material for her to make her own.

Ernest remains drunk for days at a time. He abuses the workers by beating them for not working fast enough.

One afternoon, Ernest and Prudence are sitting on the porch. Prudence is in the hammock humming and crocheting. Ernest is sitting on the steps of the house smoking a cigarette. King Bee is his favorite brand. The cigarettes have no filters—strong English cigarettes. Ernest pulls out a hundred-dollar bill and lights his cigarette with it.

Prudence looks at him and says, "You stupid English bastard. At least you can build us a better house. I'm tired of living in this damn hut. You go away for a week at a time and spend money on Spanish women and burn money!"

"It's my money, Mama," says Ernest. "I'll do what I please with it."

"At least you can buy the kids something, or bring me material to make a dress. I need a dress and material to darn your damn clothes," she says with tears trickling down her cheeks. Prudence still keeps her composure as she always does.

Carmela, the firstborn, is a beautiful, blonde, spoiled young woman. She's very outspoken and assertive, saying whatever is on her mind. She asks Ernest when he is going to take her the United States. "Daddy! Daddy! I want to go to America." Sitting in his lap, she makes faces and then turns to Prudence. "Ma, I want to go to America. Can we go to America, Ma?" she asks.

Carmela spends great amounts of time making herself pretty, and she does not mingle with the native workers. She keeps to herself and lies around the house doing nothing, just wanting to go to America.

So one day, Ernest tells her and Prudence that they are going to make a trip to America—actually, New Orleans. Carmela is bursting with excitement.

The mid-fifties come along and Ernest and Prudence have made several trips to the United States. On a visit to Miami, they are sitting around the pool sipping their drinks when a man dressed in a blue and brown plaid suit, wearing a hat and smoking a cigarette, approaches Ernest and introduces himself.

"Hello, sir," he says. "My name is Lonny, and I'm a Realtor."

Ernest says, "What is that?"

"Real estate," the man says. "I sell land. You look like a man who would be interested in land here in the United States."

"I might be interested," Ernest says.

"Yes sir, yes sir," nods the man. "I have the most perfect piece of land you've ever set your eyes on."

The next day, the same man comes by the hotel dressed in the same clothes, looking for Ernest. Ernest, Prudence, and Carmela get in the real-estate agent's car. He drives a 1950 Cadillac. Carmen is just ecstatic about being in a car. Prudence looks calm and cool as always. Lonny keeps running on about this beautiful piece of land he wants to sell.

They get to a location down the strip of Miami Beach where they get out of the car, and the Lonny shows them the land that he wants Ernest to buy.

"This is the location I want to offer you, sir. Yes sir! Yes sir! This is it—all one hundred and fifty acres. Just for you!" says the real-estate agent. "You look like a guy with lots of money who is just waiting to spend it all on something very valuable. Think about the future of this land. It can earn you more money! You go back to Utila, and you will be set for life." The real-estate agent is very persistent and seems to talk for hours.

Ernest looks down and then looks at Prudence.

Carmela is enjoying the view and the wind blowing in her face, "Daddy! Daddy! Buy this for me!" she calls out, happy and spoiled. "I want to move to the United States."

Ernest turns his head and looks at the real-estate agent. "What is your name again sir?"

"My name is Lonny! Yes sir." he says.

"You want me to buy a piece of jungle? I have a huge jungle back in Honduras," says Ernest. "You are crazy. You're out of your mind. So how much are you selling this piece of jungle for?"

The agent says, "Well sir! I will sell this to you for fifty US dollars an acre. Fifty dollars is not much. Think about all the benefits and the future of this land. It could bring you millions of dollars. Fifty dollars an acre is cheap."

Ernest turns to Prudence. "Ma! I will not buy this piece of jungle. We have a piece of jungle in Rio Tinto." Prudence gives him a gentle smile.

Back in the days before the entire strip of Miami Beach was developed, it did look like a jungle. It was full of coconut groves and tall grass and wild grape trees. At the time, who would have thought the entire strip would be developed with hotels and restaurants? The real-estate agent saw the future and the vision.

Carmela saw the vision, she was a young woman and wanted to stay and live in the States. She would beg Ernest and Prudence to let her go to live there. They had money, and they could afford to support her.

Ernest never saw the vision. He never planned for the future. He lived for today. The Lowells had money. They were known for having money and for growing coconuts by the millions. Ernest would make several more trips to Miami, New Orleans, and Tamp, but he never made any type of commitment to stay or to invest in real estate.

One afternoon, the family is sitting on the front porch. Prudence is sitting in the hammock. Carmela is sitting next to her. Ernest and his sons Ernest and Sealie are sitting on the steps. They are talking and smoking King Bee cigarettes. Carmela keeps asking Ernest when they are going to back to the States.

Carmela and her brothers Ernest and Sealie are young adults now, Carmela in her early twenties and the brothers in their late teens. Carmela keeps complaining about wanting to leave Rio Tinto, she is tired of living in a hut, and living with the mosquitos.

"Ma! Daddy! I want to go and live in the States," she says. "I love the United States. I want you to send me to the States, Ma. I want to get out of this jungle. I was not born to be in this jungle. I'm tired of living here fighting the mosquitoes and the elements," She cries. "I want to go," she says through the tears. "I'm sick of you all. I want to start my life. I will not spend my entire life in this jungle. I will not do it! You all can stay here and die here, but not me! I'm going to go to America, whether you help me or not."

"I want to live in the United States too," young Ernest says.

Sealie, sits looking cool, smoking his cigarettes, with a World War II book in his hand, says nothing. Sealie is fascinated with history, especially German history and all of those iconic figures from World War II. He will end up giving his sons and daughters the names of Nazi war criminal. He says, "Rubbish, rubbish. You are all mad. America has nothing for me. I have everything I want here on this plantation. I never want to go to the States. Everybody wants to go to America. All of you go to America, and I will die here on this bloody plantation. I wish you well!"

A few months later, Ernest, Prudence, and Carmela make a trip to Tampa to see friends. They ask their friends if Carmela can stay with them. Ernest gives the family an envelope. "This should cover you for all the trouble I'm putting you through."

Ernest and Prudence go back to Rio Tinto. Ernest goes back to his same routine of taking care of the plantation and selling coconuts by the millions. Making money is his passion.

When young Ernest—Kusa—is in Rio Tinto, people see him with a young black native women. This is something of which his parents never approve. Kusa is having an affair with one of the women in the village, but no one in his family knows. It is a big secret from the family, but everybody in the village knows. They keep the secret.

Kusa is seen coming out of a hut a few times early in the morning by some of the villagers, Negro folks who live nearby. Then, the woman has a child and the child is light-skinned black. That's how everyone in the village knows that it is Kusa's child. He denies it. They name her Vena.

Kusa swears that the child is not his. The mother's parents go to the elder Ernest and tell him that his son has had an affair with one of their daughters, got her pregnant, she bore a child, and they named her Vena.

Ernest does not accept the fact that his son would have an affair with a native Negro woman. Vena is a light-skinned baby, a very beautiful baby, and the mother is adamant that Vena is Kusa's daughter. How else would a light-skinned baby be born in a small village where there is no one but black people and dark-skinned natives? The infant also has all of Kusa's features. Everybody in the village says that she's Kusa's child. The young man does not want to accept that the child is his born of a native Negro woman.

His father does not want to accept it either. He's so furious with his son and he does not know what to do with him. Then, Kusa decides to put the blame on his brother Sealie. Kusa is not able to put the baby's paternity on Sealie, even though Kusa is insistent that she is Sealie's child, everybody in Rio Tinto knows she is Kusa's.

Ernest decides to send Kusa away to Utila until things can calm things down a bit. Kusa is no good to his father anyway. He does not want to help on the plantation. All he wants to do is sit around primping and eating. Prudence does not say anything. They have all the natives in the village working for them, so they don't need Kusa. He is lazy. He is often seen running around in the village with the young girls and kissing them. Ernest is growing tired of it. Ernest is too busy running a plantation, making money, overseeing his plantation, and supervising all the men and woman working for him to worry about what his son is getting into.

He doesn't waste any time getting rid of Kusa. Just a few days later, Juney comes for his regular coconut run, and Ernest asks Juney to take his son to Utila. Kusa is standing on the steps of the hut smoking a cigarette. His pants are rolled up knee-high, and he's looking very nervous. He knows that his father Ernest is sending him away.

As Vena grows up, everybody loves her—she is beautiful and has the features of her father and straight black hair. She becomes a very attractive young woman. She always wants Kusa to accept her as his daughter, but he refuses. It is Vena's greatest desire in life to call Kusa "father" and for Kusa to call her "daughter," but he never does.

Kusa moves to Utila, and there he gets married to a woman by the name of Emma who is a relative of Astor Hill. Emma does not love Kusa, and everybody knows this. Emma is in love with his brother Sealie. Some people on the island have seen the two of them together in a very intimate way, but Sealie does not pay the right kind of attention to her, so she marries Ernest just to be married.

Kusa is drunk a lot. When he and Emma get married, he still doesn't put the bottle away—drinking beer all the time. Kusa smokes a lot too. Even as a child Kusa smoked! The whole family smokes all the time.

So, Ernest has sent Kusa to Utila so he won't be embarrassed by the fact that his son has a child with a native woman. However, now he finds out his other son Sealie is also having an affair with a native woman. Sealie has seen staying at the woman's hut for days at a time. Sealie, now in his early twenties, is not married as of yet but is causing scandal in the family. Ernest finds out about the affair through a worker. The father of the young woman wants Ernest to support the family, but Ernest will not have anything to do with it. He confronts Sealie about the affair, but Sealie denies everything. Everybody in the small village knows of the affair, but Sealie is will not admit to it.

At this point, Ernest is going crazy. Both of his sons are having affairs with native women, and he does not know how to handle the complaints.

Soon after, a baby girl is born, and she has light skin and looks like Sealie. She has his facial features and his straight black hair. Sealie cannot deny this one, but he does, he never admits she his daughter, but she says she is, and everybody believes it.

Even after many years, this woman was always known as a Lowell. She called us her brothers and sisters. When Sealie passed away, however, she was not at the memorial. She was not aware that her father had passed away until years later. She went on with life. Today, she lives in Triunfo de la Cruz, Honduras.

Kusa having an affair with a native black woman, and Sealie having an affair with a native black woman—these things are a betrayal of the family. Ernest and Prudence just cannot handle what Kusa and Sealie have done to the family reputation. The rest of the family in Utila is not aware of what's going on in Rio Tinto. If the family were to find out, they would disown Ernest. So he keeps it very quiet. When Juney comes to buy coconuts, Ernest makes sure he does not talk to any of the workers or the natives in the village.

Sealie stays with Ernest and Prudence in Rio Tinto. He has two sons, Rommel and Pedro, and a daughter, Ester, with a Spanish woman by the name of Meradi. She's not a very attractive woman. She lives in another town called Barra de Luau. It is a small town with a huge river running through it. This very poor woman stays by herself raising his three children. Sealie rarely sees them and does not support this woman or his own children. They are never married, but they do live together from time to time until Sealie marries another woman. Meradi never meets Sealie's parents because Ernest and Prudence never approve of her. Nor do they ever acknowledge their grandchildren as Lowells.

However, at some point, they do take a liking to Rommel. Rommel is Prudence's and Ernest's favorite grandson. Even after Sealie is married and has seven "legitimate" children, Rommel remains the favorite. They spoil him, and they love him so much that they take him in. Rommel lives with them for a long time from his early teens in to his late thirties. Ester and Pedro grow up with their mother Meradi. Rommel never works in the coconut plantation. He loves being a playboy.

Rommel grows up to be a very attractive, handsome man. He has blond hair, blue eyes, and light skin. He has inherited English rather than native features. He is tall and slim. His sister Ester is also attractive, with fair skin and black hair. She looks a bit like her Spanish mother but more like her British father, Sealie. Pedro is good looking. He's Spanish-looking with darker complexion, like his mother. He is more "rough on the edges," and has a somewhat aggressive nature. Pedro has a reputation of getting into trouble in the village. Seeing Rommel with white skin, blond hair, and blue eyes, and Ester with her fair skin, Pedro resents the color of his own dark skin.

Prudence idolizes Rommel. Everything that Rommel wants, he gets. His grandparents buy jewelry, clothes, and watches for him. Because of Rommel's favor, Pedro's resentment grows deeper and deeper. He never meets his grandparents. He is not allowed to go to their house. His mother, Meradi, forbids him to go and visit. She does not like the fact that they are British and that they are wealthy. She resents the whole Lowell family because she is neither acknowledged nor supported by Prudence and Ernest. Sealie never supports them financially either, but he does acknowledge them. Pedro obeys his mother's wishes and he never meets his grandparents. Pedro grows up and goes on with his own life, farming and doing whatever it takes to survive.

Prudence nicknames Rommel "RoRo." Prudence will say, RoRo, come, dinner is ready." The favorite meal that Prudence would have the servants make for him is dumplings in coconut-milk soup.

Ester goes on with life too, but her grandparents do not acknowledge Ester either. Sealie acknowledges her, but very not much. He does not pay too much attention to her, or see her very often. Ester longs to be acknowledged by Sealie. She wants a father figure and to belong in the family. My mother acknowledged her, but did not get to know her well. Ester wanted the family name of Lowell, but Sealie did not want to give it to her. She becomes very unpredictable and insecure young woman. She joins an underground militia group and protests against the government of Honduras.

Rommel just hangs out at his grandparent's house and on the beach. Being a playboy, he is seen with a couple of the pretty young girls in the village.

One evening, Prudence is sitting in the hammock. Ernest is sitting on the porch steps. Rommel is standing next to Prudence, when suddenly she says, "Papa, I will ask Carmela if she can take Rommel to the States."

Ernest just looks at her and says, "Hush, Mama! Carmela would not take anyone to the States. Hush!"

"It wouldn't hurt to ask," says Prudence.

Rommel is so excited, "Grandma! I want to go to the States, when can I go?"

Prudence tells him, "Someday, I will write a letter to Carmela and I will ask her."

Rommel exclaims, "I want to be a merchant marine! I want to go in the cargo ships and see the world! Can I go tomorrow?"

"No, not tomorrow," says Prudence.

"Mama! I'm hungry, go fix something for lunch!" says Ernest. "You're both crazy. Hell will freeze over before Carmela helps anyone in the family. Mama, you need to get this out of your head. I will not take any letter to the post office."

Prudence soon writes the letter to Carmela and gives it to Sealie to mail. A few months later, Prudence receives a letter back from Carmela. She opens it, reads it, but she does not know how to read well, so she reads the letter slowly, word by word. Carmela says that she has started papers for Rommel to join her in the States.

A few months later, Ernest and Prudence board their sailboat and travel to Tela to take Rommel to the airport. There, he boards a plane to the United States. Prudence is so sad to see him go she can't stop sobbing. Ernest seems content, not an emotion on his face.

So Ernest and Prudence return to Rio Tinto. There they continue living in the same way, but now, with Rommel gone, it seems like Prudence is always sad.

And, life goes on . . . Ernest is still selling lots of coconuts, making lots of money, and burning it too. It does not seem to bother Prudence—living very primitively despite their wealth.

Carmela has a one-bedroom apartment in the northern part of Philadelphia. She lives very modestly, without a whole lot of furniture. She has a sofa bed, where Rommel sleeps, and a small kitchen. It is now the mid—to late '60s. She comes home every night to make dinner for herself and Rommel. She fights with him because he does nothing to help her. Ernest and Prudence do not support her, nor do they send any money to support Rommel.

Rommel lives with his Aunt Carmela for several years, and he never changes one bit. He's very demanding, and all he wants to do is lie around the house and be waited on. Carmela irons his shirts and pants so that every day that he goes to college, his clothes are neatly pressed. Carmela does that every day after her shift at the factory.

Rommel is very rebellious, and he does not want to do anything. He comes home and from school and goes out with his friends. Carmela grows impatient with him. She threatens, "Rommel, if you do not straighten yourself out, I will ship you with a one-way ticket back to Rio Tinto!"

But Rommel does not worry about it. He goes on doing his own thing. Carmela keeps catering to him by ironing his clothes, making sure his ties are pressed, and his shoes are polished every night before she goes to bed. She does it all for this grown man. He does is nothing to help her.

Finally, Carmela has had enough. She makes good on her threat and buys him a one-way ticket to Honduras—back to Rio Tinto. Rommel goes back to living with Ernest and Prudence. He goes on doing nothing, not even helping on the coconut plantation. A few months later, he goes to San Pedro Sula and signs up to join the merchant marines.

After a few months of waiting, Rommel gets his orders. He is to report at the port in Panama City. He leaves Rio Tinto and boards a plane for Panama City. He arrives in Panama, and he waits forty-eight hours for his ship to arrive. One evening, he goes out to a club, starts drinking, and he starts a fight.

The police arrive as everybody is fighting in the bar. Bottles and chairs are being thrown across the bar, and Rommel is looking to get out, but he cannot. The police have the club surrounded. Rommel gets taken away in handcuffs. They put him in the police wagon and take him to the station.

The next day, they let him out of his cell and take him to the front office. There, he meets a very attractive detective. She goes over his case, and they start a conversation. He tells her his side of the story. He talks very sweetly to the woman, and she drops all the charges against him.

He arranges to meet her later in the evening at a local bar. He walks into the bar and waits for her. The woman is Maria Lopez. She tells him about her life and that she has a child by a previous marriage. Some of the patrons just look at the blond-haired guy sitting with this brunette woman. One of the drunken men walks over to the table where Rommel and Maria are sitting.

The drunken man says, "Hey Blondie! Hey Blondie! You American? What are you doing here?"

Rommel says, "Look, man! I do not want any trouble with you. I'm just having a drink with my friend."

The drunken man says, "Do not come here anymore, okay, amigo?"

Rommel says, "Whatever, man!"

Maria just looks on, not saying anything.

The drunken patron just walks away, mumbling.

Rommel tells Maria that he's meeting a ship from Germany in Panama City. He's got to leave in the morning.

Later that evening, they walk to her apartment, and they spend the night together. When she wakes up in the morning, she finds Rommel gone. She notices a note stuck to the mirror telling her, "Thank you for the great time, but I have to leave. Take care. I will see you someday."

Rommel arrives at the ship, where he meets the captain and the rest of the men. Rommel makes himself comfortable as usual. The next day, they set sail for Germany with the cargo. He keeps busy writing to Prudence and doing his work around the ship and working with the other men.

After a few weeks traveling, the ship finally arrives in Germany. Rommel goes ashore to go sightseeing and out to the bars and clubs. After a few days in Germany, they travel to Spain. They spend a few days in Spain.

There, Rommel meets a young woman by the name of Rosa, a very attractive woman with black hair and attractive features. She is a secretary at a local bank. They get together for a few drinks. They seem to be happy with each other. He moves in with her in her small apartment and spends a few months in Spain, and later he finds out that she is pregnant with his child.

Rommel freaks out and refuses to accept that the child as his. He goes into a rage, throwing things around the apartment. Rosa is in the corner of the room, sobbing, afraid of Rommel in all his rage. The police come and try to calm him. They put him in handcuffs, and they ask Rosa if she wants them to take him away. She nods her head, yes.

The police escort Rommel out of the apartment. They take him to the police station where they fingerprint him and take mug shots. Later, Rosa arrives and tells the police that she doesn't want to file any charges against and they release him. Rommel and Rosa hug and go back to her apartment.

After spending a few more months in Spain, Rommel gets a visit from the police at the apartment where he and Rosa are living. They give him a letter and tell him that he's got forty-eight hours to get out Spain for being a trouble maker and beating on his women. He looks surprised, especially because Rosa has dropped the charges and has a baby on the way. They don't know what to do. Rommel packs his duffle bag, puts his on hat and leaves.

After spending a few years in different countries like Greece, Puerto Rico, Cayman Islands, Dubai, and Kuwait, Rommel has made many enemies. In every country he has gone, he has either ended up in jail for disorderly conduct or been thrown out of the country for not being able to support his babies. He is out of control everywhere he goes. But that does not discourage him from going to the next country to cause mayhem in bars and nightclubs.

His ship then travels to the Philippines. The crew spends a few days there. The first thing they do is look for the bars and nightclubs. Rommel goes to one of the local clubs, gets drunk, and starts another fight. Everybody starts throwing bottles and chairs. Of course, the police arrive and take Rommel to the station. They tell him he's got forty-eight hours to get out of the country and they release him.

Rommel is very confident about himself—very cocky. He knows that if he ever gets into trouble, Prudence will get him out. So, he continues to do the same things all over again. Prudence has to send him money a few times when he is in jail. All he has to do is send Prudence a telegram from wherever he is, and he has the money right away.

After he has been in Greece for a few months, Rommel boards the ship that heads for Dubai. There, the authorities are waiting for him. They board the ship and serve papers to Rommel. They tell him that a woman has filed papers to charge him with abuse. They tell him that he has forty-eight hours to leave the country. They take him into custody. A few days later, they take him to the airport, and they ship him back to Honduras.

When Rommel arrives at the Honduras airport, Prudence and Ernest are there to meet him. They take him back to Rio Tinto. He does not want to work on the coconut plantation. He lies around and does nothing looking clean and pretty. This has been his life. He always depends on Prudence and Ernest. He tries going back to the ships, but no one wants to hire him. That is all he ever wanted to do. That's all he ever did. Prudence tries to talk him into doing other types of work, but he never does. So, Rommel stays on the plantation for as long as his grandparents support him. He has lots of resentment against his father, Sealie, for not treating him like a son. They never speak to each other.

Fifteen years or so later, the money starts to run out. The coconut plantation is not dead, but it is not producing as many coconuts as before. The copra business is also slowing. Ernest and Prudence don't know what to do. They have hardly any money left and all the burning of money has stopped. The coconut sheds are empty they have but a few men working for them. All of the empty sheds that once were full of coconuts and copra now sit empty and dark, with only the smell of their former contents remaining.

Ernest and Prudence sit on the porch of their hut on any given afternoon. Prudence sits in the hammock, mending her dresses, while Ernest sits on the steps, smoking King Bee cigarettes. The front lawn is white from the cigarette butts. He either thinks out loud or talks about the past with Prudence.

They do not keep track of all the land they have, so people from the outside are moving in by the river building houses and taking over the land. Ernest tries to fight them, but to no avail. Ernest just gives up and lets the people take over his land. Once you build a house on a piece of land, you can declare that land as yours and no one can come and take it from you.

Eventually, Prudence becomes sick and has to be taken away to the island of Utila for medical attention. Ernest stays in Rio Tinto, taking care the property. He is broke, all the millions that he once made long gone. Ernest can't even buy a pack of cigarettes.

A few years later, it's time for Ernest to leave Rio Tinto. The lonely empty sheds that once held millions of coconuts and the lonely dried-out tent-shaped bamboo copra structures stand outside as a reminder that it was once a sight to see. They stand as a monument to a time of prosperity. The empty corral that was once full of cattle and men buzzing up and down, working to keep up with demand, stands silent. The coconut plantation that once produced a vast amount of coconuts on any given day lies empty, as silent as the light ocean breeze that sways in the trees. The land of milk and honey no longer produces milk or honey.

Nothing can revive the trees now. They stand in isolation. They represent only a moment in Ernest's history. Now there are only memories of the golden days, when Ernest would take hundred-dollar bills and light cigarettes with them, when he would get drunk and not know which way to go on his big boat. The big boat Ernest named *Hikity*. The boat that had become the pride and joy of Ernest's drinking days now sits as part of the river's trophy collection of memories.

The plantation should have become a museum, as a reminder that this land was once rich. It was the talk of the town. But Rio Tinto would not have existed if it weren't for the United States, which would buy its products.

Poor Rio Tinto! And, poor Ernest, once the richest man in Rio Tinto, maybe in the whole of Central America—the man who built an empire from coconuts, the man who walked tall among the natives, the man who ruled with an iron fist, the man who ruled the Lowell family, the man who could have bought the entire state of Florida if it weren't for his lack of vision. He now sits broke on the steps of his hut, penniless and old, with only memories—which cannot return as reality. They are just memories.

Rio Tinto sits in silence today reminding us, the children, of those people who could have made a difference but decided against it. How sad.

When it is time for Ernest to leave Rio Tinto, there he sits, on the porch steps, smoking a cigarette and thinking. He looks old in the pair of dirty white jeans and white shirt he wore all the time. I remember coming to his house to escort him to the beach. I was about seven years old. (It was hard to tell the passage of time in this village. We had no clocks, watches, or calendars. We just went by the sun or what we thought the time and age we were.) He looked at me and did not say anything. I stood looking at him, thinking, *there's a man who once had it all. The power, now look at him.*

This is only the second time I have come to my grandfather's house. All the years we lived nearby, he never invited us to his house. He told my father Sealie not to bring his kids to his house because we were not his kind.

Now I come without an invitation to see him and to walk with him to the beach where he's going to board Juney's boat for the last time for his final trip out of Rio Tinto. Prudence is very ill in the island of Utila. Juney's boat makes its silent, final approach and drops anchor. Ernest looks surprised, as if the reality of leaving is suddenly hitting. He looks in silence down the beach to the left and then to the right then at me with tears trickling down his cheeks.

He says to me, "I had money once—lots of money. Now I'm poor, without a penny in my pocket."

He walks toward the canoe. He can barely walk now, so I have to hold on to him. Stumbling, he gets into the small canoe. Juney watches him board the and then begins to row his friend out to his boat. I stand watching as the waves break along the sides of the canoe. I watch as he boards Juney's boat. The engines start, and the heavy black smoke from the motor blow in the wind. I watch on an empty beach until the boat fades away. I think about what the future holds for my family, the empty land, empty memories, and an empty life. I slowly walk away along the narrow pathway that leads to my family's hut and the abyss of life. I feel lonely and empty. Am I to be left to continue the legacy some day? Have I nothing to look forward to except a huge coconut plantation that I do not know how to run? Even though this is only the second time I have been in my grandfather's presence, the emotions I feel are very powerful and I cry as I watch him go. Somehow, his departure has made such an impact on me that I remember the details vividly almost fifty years later.

My father spends most of his time drinking and beating my mother. So I have to run, or pretend that I'm running the plantation. If he's not beating my mother, he's beating me, or one of my other siblings.

My grandparents' big hut is full images from the stories I was told. I go looking to see where Ernest might have hid all the money I was told he had. I look under the house and I start to dig in various places, but I come out empty-handed.

I search all over. I open the huge empty sheds, but all I see when I open them is a white cloud of smoke from being tightly closed for so long. Rats are running all over the floor, eating any remaining copra. I open the sheds one by one, all the doors, all the windows. There is nothing but lumber. He might have spent lots of money building these sheds. Although I look very hard in all the places where I was told he was hiding it for safekeeping, I do not find any money. All I find are old engines from the *Hikity*, the thirty-foot boat . . . and rats, lots of them. There is no shortage of rats. They probably ate all the money.

As a kid, I was always curious about Ernest and his money. As I'm looking through the house with a lantern, in the attic and in the closets, I'm trying hard to understand why he never bought Prudence a nice dress to wear. As far as I can remember, she wore the same dress day in and day out, nothing new. She was a very simple, modest Englishwoman. I find old stuff—hoses, glass, crystal, fine china—but they never used all this stuff.

Life in Rio Tinto was totally different from most places. The weather was always hot; we had tropical rain and hurricanes. When the hurricanes blew in, it flooded under the house, which was built it on stilts six to seven feet high for that reason. The ocean washed underneath the house during bad weather too.

Whenever one of the villagers built a hut, the rest of the people helped. Some would look for good wood in the jungle for the support beams and the walls. Others would start cutting palm branches. Palm branches were the best because they were the strongest.

The process by which those branches were prepared was unique in itself. They would cut the palm or the coconut branch, and then they would find the ends of it and split it in half. Next, they'd lay it down in bundles of ten or twenty, tie the bundles with twine, and leave the bundles for about a month until they were dry. Then the men would lift one bundle, put it over one shoulder, and then pick up another bundle and put it over the other shoulder. They'd grab a stick and put it across both piles to see where they were going and for stability, and then they'd carry the bundles to the site where the house was being built. Let me tell you, this was hard, hard work.

It could take fifty to one hundred bundles of palm branches to build a hut, depending on the size of the hut. It would have a dirt floor and look like a studio apartment: one room was the kitchen and the bedroom.

In the winter it was nice and warm, and in the summer it was nice and cool. There was no running water, no bathroom. You had to go into the jungle for that, even at night. You were lucky not to be attacked by a wild boar or a tiger!

But I'm getting ahead of myself. Before I can tell you about my life in Rio Tinto, I need to go back in time, before the death of Ernest and the loss of his wealth and power, to pick up the story of Sealie, my father, and how my parents met.

Chapter 4

Sealie Malone Lowell

It's the early '50s, and the government is beginning to develop new projects. They are building new railroads and dams, and opening new roads, and rerouting rivers across the northern territories along the banana-farm regions so the interior valleys won't get flooded.

The government is hiring to complete all of these projects. Sealie does not like working for Ernest. He wants to be free and able to build a life for himself. He has heard about the jobs building rivers and railroads. He applies for one of these jobs. He talks to the foreman who is in charge of the hiring. The foreman is well aware of the Lowells and their reputation. Sealie vaguely knows the man from long ago. He is hired on the spot. Sealie is in his early twenties and trying to start out his life without his parents.

Sealie starts working for the railroad, and since he is very charismatic, it doesn't take long before he has made many friends.

One afternoon, he and his friends are having lunch at a local café. They are joking and laughing, having a good time. Sealie does not speak Spanish, but it doesn't matter because the other men speak English. They are from the island of Utila. He notices a group of local women enter the café. He asks his friends who these women are. They are all very attractive, simple women who come to buy groceries on a regular basis.

After seeing them a few times, he walks up to one of them and asks her name. She turns and smiles very prettily, not knowing how to speak English. He calls over one of his friends who speaks Spanish to translate for him.

"My name is Sealie. Sorry, I don't speak your language, Spanish."

She says, "Its okay. My name is Dolores. I live over that mountain with my parents. These are my sisters."

Sealie says, "I want to come and visit you sometime when I have time."

Dolores says, "No, you cannot! Please don't! My father will kill you if you visit me!"

Her sisters look on, giggling. Smiling, Dolores walks away toward her sisters. She turns around to see Sealie's expression.

Sealie turns to his friend, who translates, "Her father will kill you if you visit. You are a dead man if you go and visit her! So my suggestion is to stay away from her and the house. I really don't want to go and pick you up with bullets in your body!"

"Well! Well! Thank you!" says Sealie. But he doesn't take the advice.

One day, Sealie takes off from his regular job working on the railroad and he decides to go and pay this beautiful woman Dolores a visit. He walks up a steep hillside for an hour and a half. He walks past a corral full of grazing cattle. As he passes, the cows stop, turn, and watch him. After trekking for quite some time, he sees a series waterfalls and a brook that runs across a corral. He will learn later that this is where the women go to the brook to wash clothes.

Finally, Sealie comes to a house with smoke billowing from the wood-burning stove. He slowly approaches. He walks around it and sees a well, and cattle, chickens, pigs, goats, and fruit trees nearby. Some men are working, not paying attention to him, so he sneaks by and moves toward the watering hole. He hides in the bushes and waits thinking that Dolores will come to get water. So he waits and waits and waits. He fights the ants crawling all over him, around his face and up his arms. After waiting for what seems to be an eternity, he begins to doze off.

Finally, he hears voices. A group of women is approach the well. It is Dolores with her two sisters. He casually comes out of the bushes brushing the ants off his clothes. The women are startled and frightened by this stranger who has appeared from nowhere. As he introduces himself, he keeps brushing off the ants.

The women try to him to leave because their father will kill him if he is found there, but he doesn't understand Spanish. Speaking in English and gesturing with his hands, Sealing tells them that he is going to go to her father and ask permission to visit her. He helps them collect the water, and he tells them that he wants to take it to their house. They all say, "We do not want to see anyone hurt over us."

Sealie tells them that he will go, and promises that he will come back again soon. He runs across the field and among the cattle excited about the prospect of returning to see Dolores again.

Sealie continues his work for the government, building dams and rerouting the river. Six months pass, Sealie decides to go and look for Dolores. He hides in the bushes and waits by the well again. When he sees her, he steps out of the bushes. He asks Dolores if she wants to go with him. She looks frightened, but her sisters encourage her to go. Sealie takes Dolores away to the nearest city, Tela, to get married.

Dolores's sisters run home and tell their father that Dolores has gone away with a white man. Dolores's father runs out of the house and orders one the workers to saddle his horse. Her father checks his two guns for bullets and straps them to his waist. He mounts his horse, his son follows, and they ride to town where all the men are working. They look for Sealie, but Sealie is nowhere to be found.

The two men search the woods, Jungle and all over the village Rio Tinto, telling the people that if anyone sees a white gringo with blond hair to bring him to their house so they can hang him. After searching all day until sundown, they call off the search. The next day they hire a local man to search for her.

That same night, Sealie and Dolores arrive in Tela on the evening train where they go directly to the justice of the peace and ask him if he will marry them at the Hotel Tela. They set a time for him to meet them at the hotel. Sealie and Dolores go to buy a simple wedding dress. Dolores, in her new dress, and Sealie, in blue jeans and a white shirt, say their vows. There are no witnesses; it is just the two of them.

A few days later, Sealie arrives home in Rio Tinto with his new bride. From the porch, he calls out, "Papa! Mama! I'm home, and I want you to come out to the porch. I have someone I want to present to you!"

So Ernest and Prudence come to the porch. Sealie presents his new wife. They just stand there looking surprised and stunned. They do not say anything. They stare at the new couple in disbelief. Ernest takes Sealie to the side and they talk in whispers. Dolores looks down, with sadness in her eyes.

Ernest tells Sealie, "You take this damn trash of a Spanish woman out of my house and off my property, right now!"

Ernest stomps angrily to the front porch door and into the hut, slams the door so hard that it breaks. He is out of breath and angry. He goes through the hut out the back and comes around the front. "I never want to see you or her on my property, never! I have disowned you. You're a disgrace to the family and to the English people! You see this property? Do you see this damn property? I was going to pass it on to you! As of right now, Mama and I will not to give you anything!"

Sealie stares at his father in amazement. He grabs Dolores by the arm and they walk away. They go and stay with a neighbor. Dolores is very sad and can't stop crying.

A few days later, Ernest calls Sealie to the house. Sealie goes and meets with him.

"I'm so disappointed, my son, to see that you did not follow the heritage of the English people but decided to betray me and your mother by marrying a Spanish woman. A nobody!" Sealie strokes his eyebrows, listening. "Mama and I have changed our minds and decided to give you part of the plantation so you can live and support your damn woman! I will give you San Jose. I can't go through my life regretting my actions."

Sealie stops stroking his eyebrows and looks very intently at Ernest. San Jose has one hundred and fifty acres, and stretches from one end of the town to the other.

"It will be sufficient for you to survive and feed your woman!" says Ernest. "But I do not—do not!—want you to set foot in my house with that damn Spanish woman! I also do not want any children that you are going to have with this woman to set foot in my house! You get this through your head! San Jose is big enough for you to support her and yourself, so you will no need my help anymore! So go! Right now!"

Ernest hands Sealie the deed to the property.

Sealie walks away with the papers. As he leaves, Ernest turns and kicks the open the front door. Sealie hears him yell, "Mama! I do not want to see this man in my house again! As far as I'm concerned, he does not exist in our life!

He has betrayed us, the English people and is an insult to every Englishman and to the queen!"

Ernest goes on making money. He continues to light his cigarettes with hundred-dollar bills. It is a practice he is known for and he enjoys it.

Sealie lives in San Jose with Dolores. He becomes very successful with his part of the plantation. Now Ernest has a competitor for coconuts. Sealie is producing more than a million coconuts a month, and he is selling coconuts to Juney at twenty cents a coconut, cheaper than Ernest. Every time Juney comes to buy coconuts, he goes to Sealie first.

Juney brings his sack full of money and does business with Sealie first and then buys the rest of what he needs from Ernest. It is a major production when the coconuts are being transported from San Jose to the boat. The men, more than fifty, line up, each with a sack of coconuts, hauling them on their shoulders. Each sack holds between fifty and seventy-five coconuts, depending on how strong the men are. They work for Sealie and he pays them anywhere between one dollar and a dollar and a half a day. The workers love making so much money. What a sight it is!

Ernest now sees Sealie as a rival in coconut industry. It builds an even bigger resentment between them. Ernest decides that he wants to take San Jose back from Sealie. He tells Sealie that one way or another he will take back the land even if has to burn all the trees to the ground. Years later, feuding over San Jose, Prudence tells Sealie that Ernest has had a change of heart, that Ernest was so angry he was getting ready to burn the plantation along with the house, but decided to let it go.

For years Ernest does not talk to Sealie. He tries hard to compete with Sealie in coconut production. Sealie does not have any cattle while Ernest does. Sealie doesn't want anything to do with Ernest. He goes on selling coconuts, and lots of them. Money is flowing like water from a waterfall for Sealie.

On the other side of town, there live two families. They are from San Salvador, and they have large herds of cattle. They come to town every day to sell their milk, cheese, and bread. We buy from them frequently. Our house is the first stop. We know the entire family. They are very personable. Dolores has their kids stay over sometimes when they stay late selling milk. The boy is around fifteen years old, and he comes with the father.

One day, they come to sell milk, we buy from them, and Dolores invites them to have breakfast. They have breakfast that morning, and they go on their way to the village selling their milk. Later that afternoon, we see them riding their horse's home. We wave as they go by, and they wave also.

We think it's just another day, but later we are listening to the radio and it says that war has broken out between Honduras and El Salvador. The troops are advancing into El Salvador; we keep listening to the news. The only station that the elder Sealie listens to is Radio Belize. It comes in very clearly.

The following day, early in the morning, it is drizzling. We hear a knock on the kitchen door. It's the boy who sells milk with his father, crying. He tells us someone had assaulted and killed his parents along the river as they were going home the previous night. He describes the horrible assault by one of the men from the village. The boy is crying, sobbing and trembling. His mother was expecting a child. He is afraid of what has happened. He goes home. We watch him walking, crying, along the coconut plantation. We are afraid for him.

Later that day he comes back, crying and trembling even more. He's wet. It's still raining. He sits down in a chair, and he starts to tell us what has happened. He says that they found his mother floating in the river, all cut up. He tells us he was hiding in the bushes and watched as his father hid in a well, came out, and then swam across the river to pull his wife out of the water, when he was killed with a machete.

That day is hard for all of us, to hear what happened to this family. The rest of the family is now afraid to go out of the house for fear of being assaulted or killed by someone who does not like people from El Salvador because of the war. We never see them again. They leave the village. All of their cattle are left behind. The family thinks we should buy them, but my father Sealie does not agree.

Sealie, at this time, is starting to get sick. He has been feeling ill but he never tells anyone. He drinks a great deal and smokes excessively. He drinks water that's full of bacteria and oil. As he works on the plantation, he sometimes vomits blood and has pains in his upper back rib cage.

Ernest takes Sealie on his boat to see doctors in the city. They never find out what's ailing Sealie. They go to see the best doctors, but to no avail. As Sealie gets worse, Dolores does not know how to treat him or what to do for him. She does not know how to speak English, and he does not know how to speak Spanish.

Prudence sends the elder Sealie's sister Carmela an urgent telegram, asking her to consider taking Sealie to the States to see the doctors there. If he doesn't go, he will die. A few months go by and there's nothing from Carmela. Finally, after six months, Prudence receives a telegram stating that Carmela is getting the papers ready for Sealie to come to the States.

Eight more months go by, and finally, Prudence gets the papers from Carmela for Sealie to go to the States. At first he refuses to go, but he finally does. His problem is that he does not want to accept help from his sister.

Prudence, not wanting to go to Sealie's house—not wanting to see Dolores—asks Sealie to go to her house and stay a few days before he leaves for the States. There was a time when Sealie was not welcome in his parents' house, but with time, Ernest has forgotten his threats. Now Sealie packs his bags. Ernest and Prudence have him stay for a couple of days and they take Sealie to the airport and put him on a plane to the States. Carmela has paid for the plane ticket and all of the expenses.

Carmela gets Sealie admitted to the University of Pennsylvania Hospital in Philadelphia. The city is a very shocking thing for Sealie. He does not like living in the city, he feels out of place. He is so used to the jungle and picking coconuts that he cannot wait until he returns. Living with Carmela is also difficult for him. Sealie does not like her bossing him around and telling him what to do. She spends most of her time taking him to doctors and to the hospital.

After about six months, the doctors determine that the problem is with Sealie's liver. They diagnose him with cirrhosis of the liver from drinking too much alcohol and also drinking the water from the village. The doctors tell him that if he does not boil his drinking water and stop drinking and smoking, he will die. But the well water from the village is contaminated with bacteria. There is a film of oil that floats on the surface. Tadpoles can be seen swimming down below. And, that is the water all the villagers drink. There is no other water.

Sealie heads back to Rio Tinto. At first, he boils his drinking water, but it's not long before he goes back to his old routine. He's drinking the regular water without boiling it, continues drinking and smoking heavily.

Sealie's health takes a heavy toll on his wife. Dolores begs him to stop drinking, and he does not listen. His answer is that all the treatment in the States was nothing but hogwash. Doctors are nothing but hogwash. He goes on drinking his beer and smoking. Every time Juney comes and buys coconuts from him, he goes away for a week to the city to drink and spend money on women.

There is a man from another town who comes to sell merchandise and supplies, and Sealie befriends him. He looks like a nice guy. Every time this guy comes, Sealie says to me, "Go and bring us a beer!"

I gladly go and get beers for the both of them.

By the time the beer gets to them, half of it is gone because I drank it. They both get drunk while talking and telling stories. Dolores makes dinner, and I go and pick coconuts in the middle of the afternoon. I'm drunk too.

I do not care. I do not feel the mosquitoes biting me or, the wasps stinging me. I come home later that day with my lips and eyes all puffed up from being bitten or stung. Sometimes I would come home with a snake around my neck because I did not feel it. I think it's funny, laughing my head off, seeing a snake around my neck. I say, "Nice snake!" And then I pass out. It's a distraction from the boredom of life and the misery of picking coconuts.

One time I'm standing next to a coconut tree looking up. I go to lean against it, and suddenly I feel something squeezing me tight. I do not know what it is. The next thing I know, a boa constrictor is wrapped around me, and the trunk of the tree. I'm totally stuck to the coconut tree! This thing is huge! I scream so loud and I scream again. I think it's going to swallow me. I see his head, the size of a coconut, coming at me. I cannot breathe. I start to pass out. The next thing I feel is the wetness of the snake's blood running down my chest. Sealie has come and cut the head off the snake. I gasp for air. We take the snake home and eat it. That is a meal and a half. I feel like bait. I did something good for a change. I'm proud of myself.

Sealie decides he wants a boat so; he goes to Roatan and places an order for a custom-made boat—a fifty-foot sailboat. A year later, he goes back to Roatan and picks up the boat, which he names *Swan Roatan*. What a sight to see! It is such a nice boat! Sealie takes a few pictures posing next to his boat in Roatan before sails back to Rio Tinto. In the pictures he looks very happy with a smile on his face. You rarely see Sealie with a smile. He's always very serious. In later years, when Sealie shows the pictures to a well-trusted friend, his friend takes the pictures and never brings them back.

When the *Swan Roatan* has the two sails up and the wind in its sails, it is a sight to see. It's an awesome boat, and fast. Sealie seems to have fun with it. He spends most of his time painting it and building a nice mahogany deck. All the villagers are very jealous of Sealie when they see his boat.

One time he takes me on his boat to Puerto Cortes. I am so excited about going, but I'm afraid because I know that he will get drunk and we will get lost at sea.

We get to Puerto Cortes. Its evening and the city lights are so pretty. I am amazed that there is a world out there—a pretty world, at that!

I'm sleeping below deck, and it's hot. Sealie asks me to come and sleep with him on deck. I go on deck and he starts showing me the stars. There is bright moonlight. The moon is so big. I have never seen the moon like this before. It is a new world!

After a few days in Puerto Cortes at the place he hangs out, he goes on a drinking spree. It's the day we're ready to set sail for home. I am scared to board the boat because he's so drunk. He can't even stand up. A few men have to carry him on board. I remember looking at the city as it fades away in the distance as we sail away. I am frightened. There is no wind, and Sealie cannot steer the boat. He's slumped over the tiller. I just watch for a while and it comes to a point, about five in the evening, where we're not moving. It seems as though we're going in circles. I don't know what to do and the other passengers, about five of them, don't know what to do either.

So finally Sealie says, "Okay, we need to let you all off here."

I'm thinking, *Where am I? I don't know where I am. It looks like another village to the south of Rio Tinto. These waters are shark infested. We have a small canoe to get to shore, two at a time. If we get off, we have too far to walk. If we stay, the ocean is very still, no wind, and it's going to get dark soon. Here we are in the middle of the ocean with a drunk at the tiller.*

Some of the men lower the small canoe, and we go to shore two by two. We have to walk almost twenty miles to get home. Sealie stays on board the boat. I look at the boat going in circles and Sealie slumped against the steering tiller. What a sight to see. Sad.

When Sealie finally comes home, something sets him off and he starts beating Dolores. I'm listening to everything being thrown in the kitchen and the noise of the belt hitting her skin. It almost sounds like a whistle. This beating is bad. I listen from my bed with the covers over my head, covering my ears with my hands, trembling, hoping that it would end soon. I remember hearing the sound of his belt hitting flesh, and Dolores screaming and crying, begging him to stop.

Sealie would beat Dolores for nothing, because the food was cold or if she didn't cook what he liked. Sometimes Dolores would go and spend time with her parents at their cattle ranch just to get away from Sealie. She would leave me home with my father and take the rest of the kids with her. She would spend several weeks at a time with her parents. He lets her go, but when she comes back, it is to another big fight. I stay with Sealie, and he does not cook, he just spends most of his time on the plantation. For dinner, he serves sardines in oil from the can. What a horrible dinner!

Sealie does not want to follow the doctors' orders. He has always thought that doctors are a waste of time. He is getting sicker and sicker. Despite Sealie's health and the abuse he perpetrates on Dolores they keep having Children. Their first-born is Carmela—Sealie names her after his sister. Carmela is born with fair skin, blue eyes, and blonde hair like her father. The second is Saina. She looks like Dolores with dark skin and very curly hair. She has Spanish features. I am the third is a son Sealie. I have dark hair and skin also. George, Janelle, and Jacinta follow in that order. They all have their mother's native coloring. Growing up, we were all jealous of Carmela; we wanted to be like her, look like her. Carmela did not get along with us because she looked so different than the rest of us.

Sealie gives his firstborn illegitimate son with Meradi the name Rommel after World War II German Field

Marshal Erwin Rommel and me the middle name Von Kleist, after Nazi war criminal Paul von Kleist.

Sealie continues to make frequent trips to Puerto Cortes. He goes for a week or so at a time. He comes back drunk and not able to steer the boat properly, not knowing where he is at sea. He gets lost frequently.

As Sealie's drinking problem gets worse, he gets more violent with Dolores. Every time he comes home drunk, he abuses Dolores. He beats her so hard that sometimes she spends days unable to get up out of bed. This goes on for years, the abuse of Dolores and most of the kids. The beatings that he gives Dolores are unbelievably horrible, yet she does nothing about it. She takes all of his beatings and his erratic behavior.

Juney is making more frequent trips to Rio Tinto to buy coconuts; Sealie has stored coconuts under his house to protect them from the elements. He doesn't have sheds like Ernest, so the coconuts get stored under the hut that is built high on stilts. Juney comes with a burlap sack full of money, all in dollars, not in pesos. The next day after Juney's visits, Sealie makes plans to go to the city, drink, and spend money on women. He always stays about a week at a time.

I am the one picking coconuts while he is away. Sealie comes back a week later, drunk, sometimes not able to steer the boat; or he passes Rio Tinto. We see the boat *Swan Roatan* approach Rio Tinto and then watch it go by.

When Sealie goes to the city, he never brings the family anything, not even a pack of gum or a toy for the kids. Oh yes, one time he brings us a cola to drink on a Saturday night. It is such a treat! We feel loved. We always wonder what happens to all those burlap sacks full of money. Maybe he puts them in the bank in Puerto Cortes, but who are we to ask him about his money?

I'm afraid of living in our house. I feel very uneasy there. Things happen at night, and during the day too, that no one can explain. There are noises in the rooms like walls being punched, things being thrown—very weird, scary things.

We live near a cemetery, and when I go and pick coconuts, I always have to pass by this cemetery. It freaks me out, looking at the lonely tombstones as I go by and remembering the stories that Rommel has told me, and the stories that Dolores and Sealie tell us of things that happen there, bad things.

I become afraid to sleep at night. That is why I wrap myself in the sheets, leaving a lantern on low all night. Every time I hear the horns of the ships passing by at night, I feel safe. That means there are people around. We are in bed at eight every night. Sometimes I hate to go to bed because I'm afraid of the night and what could happen while we're asleep.

There is much tension between Sealie and his two sons from Meradi. Rommel and Pedro. Pedro does not bear the family name; only Rommel has the Lowell name. No one acknowledges Pedro as part of the family.

There is a lady by the name of Tomasa, a businesswoman. She comes to sell plantains. She likes the fact that there is so much land by the river. So she goes and asks Ernest if she can borrow or rent a small parcel of the land to set up a fish business.

Ernest, as ungenerous as he usually is, says yes. He gives her about an acre of land next on the riverbank so she can set up a fish market. All the fishermen come to her to sell their catch on a daily basis. She is buying large quantities of fish. It seems to be a very profitable and rewarding business.

When Sealie finds out that his father Ernest gave this woman a piece of land to set up her own business, he becomes furious. He goes and asks Ernest why and Ernest tells him off and sends him away, adding more to the family hostilities.

Rommel goes to work for Tomasa buying fish. He gets very involved in the business and he treats it as if it were his own. Rommel brings Pedro to work for Tomasa also. Sealie soon finds out that his sons are working for this woman; he is very upset.

Rommel orders the ice for the fish market and picks it up from the train station. The train station is about a five-hour ride in a canoe east, upriver. There are many small villages along the way, and they all seem to be dangerous. Rommel goes and picks up the immense blocks of ice for the business. Each block must have weighed a couple hundred pounds. He sends Pedro when he cannot make it. This lady's fish business is booming!

A few months later, Sealie decides that he is going to open a fish business a few yards from Tomasa's. He builds a fish hut about a hundred yards downriver from her. It's a better location because it's where the river runs into the ocean. It's easier and more convenient for fisherman to sell their fish here. Sealie gets six, three-foot by two-foot, ice coolers, and goes to the city of Tela. He orders enough to fill the coolers.

Rommel gets angry. He thinks that Sealie is being spiteful and trying to drive Tomasa out of business. Rommel and Sealie have choice words. One day, Rommel goes to Sealie's house and they have it out. I hear them screaming at each other in English. I don't understand English so I can't make much out of the arguing. Finally, I hear the back door slam. Rommel has left the house. My heart is pounding; from the sound of it, I knew it had to be bad.

At this point, Sealie is delivering thousands of fish to his distributors. They are happy and he is making more of money. Tomasa's fish business is starting failing. She is still buying and selling, but not as much as she was before Sealie set up shop.

I, young Sealie, go and help my father at the fish market, just to be there and keep him company and to look after the store while he goes home to eat.

One day, Sealie has an overwhelming amount of fish. He does not know how to keep it fresh. He orders more ice from the ice company in Tela to be delivered to the train station, but he cannot go and get the ice because he is too sick to paddle five hours up river against the river's strong current.

He knows that Rommel and Pedro are going that day to pick up ice for Tomasa. He goes to Rommel and Pedro and asks them, being that they are going to pick up their ice, if they would wait another hour to pick up his two tons of ice. He will pay them for their time and travel. Rommel and Pedro agree that they will do him this favor, just this one time.

Rommel and Pedro get in their small, motor-powered canoe around midnight. They get to the train station about six in the morning. The train pulls into the station, they unload the ice for Tomasa's business, and the train pulls away. An hour later, the other train pulls in, and they unload the ice for Sealie. Rommel and Pedro put Sealie's ice blocks in front of the canoe so it won't get mixed up with their own ice. They wrap the ice well so it won't melt, and they head home downriver.

I don't know how this went down, but Rommel and Pedro start to talk about Sealie, how bad he is and how very spiteful it is that he opened a fish market next to Tomasa's. As they continue to about Sealie, they get angrier. Rommel hands a machete to Pedro who cuts the rope from the tarps covering Sealie's ice. Rommel slows the boat's engine, walks over, removes the tarps, and starts dumping all of the ice into the river; block after block after block.

With all that ice in the river, the blocks look like icebergs floating in Alaska. Rommel and Pedro are laughing hysterically. They cannot contain themselves.

When they get home, Sealie is waiting for his ice. They walk up to him and tell him what they have done.

Rommel says to him, "We dumped your damned ice in the river, old man! You want your ice? It's floating in the river. Go and pick up your own damn ice." He and Pedro laugh in Sealie's face.

You can imagine the look on Sealie's face and his reaction. He is so damn mad; he wants to kill both of them at that moment! But he keeps his cool. Sealie walks to his shop and starts throwing all his fish in the river. Rommel, watching, from his canoe in the river, laughs. Sealie dumps all the fish in the river and sets his store ablaze. He stands watching his fish market burning.

Sealie goes home and walks to a closet. He opens it and pulls out a gun. Dolores stops Sealie from returning to the fish market and killing Rommel and Pedro.

Sealie does not see or hear from is sons Rommel and Pedro for almost five years. To make things worse, their sister Ester comes to visit Sealie after being out of touch for a few years. She has joined an underground group to overthrow the government. She comes to the house to visit and brings along about six hard-looking militiamen. She wants Sealie to make room for all of them. Sealie says no, and they get into a huge argument.

Sealie tells her to stay out of his house. These guys look mean, as if they have just come out of a fight. They are covered with machete cuts from their faces and necks to their arms. Ester, though, is still attractive. She's brunette, with striking facial features and a nice figure. She's young, in her mid-twenties by this time.

They set up tents outside the house. It looks like a small tent city. They are all wearing military fatigues. Even Ester is dressed in fatigues. She walks and talks with the kids while Sealie is picking coconuts. As kids, I guess we are fascinated to see her and these guys dressed in their military clothing, but we know not to get too close to her because Sealie has told us she is nothing but trouble.

Esther's problem with Sealie is that he did not give her his last name. That is Pedro's issue also. I guess she has come to claim her last name, but it does not work. Sealie cannot wait for her to go. He feeds her and her friends, but that is all.

That is the last time we see Ester. We hear that she is killed in a battle fighting to overthrow the government. We hear this from Francisco. She fights hard, but she and the rest of her comrades are killed. She never gets her last wish—to get to know our father.

Carmela, Sealie's sister, makes a trip to Rio Tinto to visit their parents Ernest and Prudence. We all have heard she is coming from the United States. As kids, we are fascinated to see her. We have heard that she has blonde hair and wears pants. Sealie doesn't like women wearing pants. A woman coming to his house in pants is a great sin. Except for Ester in her fatigues, we have never heard of a woman wearing pants, especially in Rio Tinto. This will be a great event!

It is a sunny day and Sealie is expecting her to visit him because she wants to see the kids. Sealie has warned us not to get too close to her because she's crazy. We are looking forward to seeing her no matter what Sealie says. He tells us what time to expect her and to close all the doors of the house because he does not want to see her. So, we close all the doors and windows and pretend that no one is home. Sealie leaves the house and goes to pick coconuts.

We have a small store in front of the house, and there is a small hole under the counter against the north wall. From it, we are able to see the town. So I run to the front of the store and start looking through the small hole to see her. I want to see her, especially her blonde hair. It's not every day that we get to see people from the outside in this village, especially from the United States, what a great thing!

I'm looking through the hole and suddenly I see a white woman with blonde hair. I run and tell Dolores that Aunt Carmela is here. All the kids run toward the front of the house because they want to see her too. They all take turns looking through the small hole.

Carmela is wearing colorful pants with high heels and a white top. Her pants look like a rainbow of color, plaid and very bright. We are fascinated by her blonde hair. Dolores remains sitting in the living room while Carmela is at the bottom of the steps. Carmela calls for Sealie three times, but Sealie is not in the house. He has made himself busy.

After a few minutes of calling for Sealie, Carmela turns around and goes back to her parents' house. She stays a few days visiting Ernest and Prudence, but Sealie never goes to visit her, and she never comes back. That is the last time we see her.

Sealie has a trip planned with one of his friends. They are going to catch a train to go to the city of Tela. They get up around midnight so they can be at the train station by seven in the morning in Sealie's small canoe. One of the villagers takes them. Sealie does not trust most of the villagers. Every time he goes with one of them to catch a train, Sealie sits in the back of the canoe, never in the front, in case they want to do something to him.

Sealie keeps to himself most of the time. He never gets too close to anyone in the village. He's always by himself. It's one of the things people in the village cannot understand. But, there is one man in the village who Sealie trusts—Nando Licona. Sealie only talks to him. Nando speaks a bit of English because he used to live in the United States, so he learned the language.

One time around midnight, there is a knock on the kitchen door because Nando Licona has a trip planned. He tells Sealie he is not going on the trip because there is tons of cut lumber floating in Punta Sal (the Atlantic Ocean) from a ship that sank.

Sealie and Nando head over to see all this lumber. They get in the small canoe and start paddling toward Punta Sal. There they find the sea covered with lumber so they start gathering all they can get their hands on.

Before sunrise, the villagers are there gathering their portions of lumber. Some are tying lumber together and climbing on top and paddling to shore. A few fights break out from people stealing each others lumber. Some get into fights with machetes and a few get killed.

Sealie gets his share; he also buys what he can. Sealie wants the lumber because he has a vision that someday he will move to the island of Utila, build a house, and live there. Dolores does not want to go to the islands. She does not want to live far away from her parents.

Sealie gets so much lumber that there's enough to build several big houses. He puts all that lumber under Ernest's house and in his empty sheds. But not all of it fits in the sheds so he leaves some of it outside. He stays up at night guarding it to make sure no one steals it. A few times people sneak around the back and try to take it, but Sealie catches them and beats them up with his machete. So the thieves walk, or limp, home after the beating that Sealie gives them.

Like those thieves, the lumber Sealie fights to gather will come to a bad end. But that is much further on in my tale. I have told stories of my great-grandfather, my grandfather, and my father. Now it is time to tell stories of my own.

CHAPTER 5

Young Sealie

I'm five years old, living in a small village that seems very far away from everything. You cannot see anything on the horizon, just a huge body of water that is the Atlantic Ocean. In this place, nothing goes out, and nothing comes in from the other world. I call it the *other world* because we do not see people from other places.

I'm sure there are people out there in the other world, but my world is a very lonely place—nothing to see, nothing to smell, just the ocean. You look to the north and all you see is a huge mountain with a river running alongside of it. You look to the south and all you see is another big mountain with a river running alongside of it too.

The beach is covered with white sand and along the shore are different sized canoes. It's a long beach with green shrubs and lots wild grapevines growing along the entire length of the beach. Coconut trees serve as a buffer between the ocean and the village. The village is small, about five hundred people, mainly African natives. They do not speak Spanish. They only speak their native language called Garifuna. They are a unique people because they are the descendants of slaves, Luther brought them to Rio Tinto, and they stayed.

I'm the third born in a family of seven children. We are one of only two white families in this village—my grandfather's family, who live at the other side of the village, and us. My Grandfather, and my father are British. As for us the kids, we all have dark skin like our Honduran mother, except for our sister Carmela.

We live on the south end of the village. My grandfather has a huge coconut plantation, about fifteen hundred acres. My father has about a hundred and fifty acres of plantation that my grandfather gave to him.

The south end of the village where we live is called San Jose. It is a decent place to live, but it is not a great place to live. There are better places, I imagine. Our home is made out of lumber, old-looking with no paint, just your typical square-looking hut. It has wood-framed windows and big wooden doors, and it sits up on ten-foot coconut-tree stilts. From the ground to the hut there are ten to fifteen steps made out of wood. It is that high because we live about a thousand feet from the ocean. When we have hurricanes, the ocean rushes under the house.

At night it gets very dark. The bright stars up in the sky provide a bit of light to the dark lonely nights we have here. The moon is very bright also. When we have a full moon, it is almost like daytime. All the houses in the village are huts made out of palm leaves with dirt floors and on stills.

If you look any direction from our house, you see nothing but jungle and coconut trees—coconut trees to the right and coconut trees to the left. You wake up in the morning and all you hear is the sound of monkeys feeding and looking for food in the jungle nearby. If you look to the west, you see Punta Sal and the Atlantic Ocean. You wash dishes in the evening and in front of you there is nothing but thick jungle. Monkeys jump along coconut trees. Lots of bad snakes look at you, sticking their tongues out while you're washing the dishes from dinner, wishing they could have you for their dinner.

After sunset, all the night creatures come out to play: monkeys, deer, and tigers. They come out and look for anything and anyone to eat. They come to the steps of the house, searching for food. Every day, I get up and eat some breakfast. I do not look forward to picking coconuts, but I know there is no way out.

My mother, Dolores, tries to send me to school. I walk to school, which is a small hut nearby. But I don't stay in school and finish the day. I tell the teacher I have to go and pick coconuts. The teacher lets me go; it's a way of life in the village.

The schoolhouse is a small, also on high coconut-tree stilts. It has fifteen steps from the ground to the door. It's high, and you can get sick just going up or going down. We have uniforms, sort of: white shirts and dark blue pants for the boys, dark blue skirts and white tops for the girls. If you can't afford that, you just come in your dirty shorts and your dirty shirt. School starts at eight in the morning, and we form a line outside the schoolhouse.

Everybody is very quiet. The teacher, who the government sends to the village to teach us, makes us line up and walks in back of us to make sure we are behaving. Then he walks in front of us, looking at our appearance, making sure we are clean and neat for the school day. Some of us are not so clean, sometimes. We have no nice clothes. Those who have good clothes, or clean uniforms, are the ones who have relatives in the States. They buy the kids their uniforms in the States and send them to the village. It takes about three months for anyone to get anything in the village.

The teacher makes us put our hands out. He walks to each of us and makes us extend our hands for inspection. The teacher walks around with a ruler in his hand, inspecting each and every one of us. He is so picky about the cleanliness of our hands. It's unbelievable. He makes us extend our hands, he inspects the front then he makes us turn our hands to the other side. If he sees that your hands are dirty, he makes you turn your hands to the front, he grabs his ruler, and he smacks your hands really hard.

When the teacher smacks your hands, he does not smack the palm of your hand, he smacks your fingers. Believe me, it hurts! If you cry, he takes you out of the line, grabs a stick that he has nearby, and gives you a spanking really hard. He lifts your skirt to do it if you are a girl. And if you're a boy you have to pull your pants down. Then he makes you get back in line. No one is allowed to look at or make fun of the person who is being disciplined. These inspections take so long, and you're just standing in line.

One day, he walks to me. There I am, with my hands extended, looking serious and straight ahead, being quiet, not breathing, holding my breath until he passes me. I see him walking to me out of the corner of my eyes. I'm holding my breath, hoping that he won't find anything wrong with my hands, but I know he will. He strolls over to me. He looks at me and then at my hands and my fingernails. They are bad, very bad, let me tell you! I chew my fingernails when I am hungry or when I am nervous. He looks at my hands, he makes me turn them over to the other side, and I hesitantly do so. Then he walks around in back of me, checking my uniform. But I have no uniform. I'm dressed in shorts and an old shirt. My shorts are just about falling down and I have no belt.

He asks me, "Why are you not in uniform?"

I tell him that I have no uniform.

"And why not?" he asks. "Who are your parents? I need to go and pay a visit to your parents."

"Yes, teacher!" I say.

He has long fingernails. He grabs the back of my neck with his fingers and then he slides his nails along my neck leaving big scratches. It hurts and I cannot make a sound. I'm in pain, tears in my eyes, and I'm still standing there with my hands extended. He walks in front of me again and smacks my fingers with his ruler. I'm in a lot of pain. I don't know how to describe how it feels when someone smacks you on your fingers with a stick. He hits hard, as if he enjoys it, and I think he does.

We are not to say anything or do anything, just stand there in pain. The other kids are not to look at you or say anything, just stand there as if nothing is going on. After an hour or so of inspections, he makes us run up the steps to the classroom, it's one huge room. There are three different grade-levels of students.

By this time, we're so sore from all the smacks he has given us with his ruler that we cannot hold the pencils or even open our notebooks to copy homework from the blackboard. He calls us individually to walk to the blackboard, and he tells us what to write and what to add and subtract. I don't know how to add or subtract, but if he would ask how many coconuts are in fifty plus fifty, I would know how many. That I would know really fast.

Instead, he picks odd numbers for us to subtract or to add. If you do not know how to add or to subtract, he makes you go outside of the classroom and kneel down in the sun. He puts a two-foot board covered with tiny stones on the ground, and he makes you kneel on top of that. A grater is a board with lots of tiny stones embedded in the board, it is used to grating coconuts. When the sun hits the grater, it gets really hot, believe me. Your knees start baking after an hour of kneeling on top of that!

When you get up from kneeling for so long on top of the stone grater, your knees are so red and the indentations from the tiny stones are embedded deep. Your knees are so sore you cannot stand up straight, and then you are sent home.

I get home, carrying my notebook with nothing written in it, and my mother asks me, "What happened in school today?"

I say, "Nothing." She notices my red knees and says nothing about them, but she says to me, "Go pick coconuts."

Not wanting to go and pick coconuts after a hard time in school; with my sore, red knees, I walk away slowly. I look for my machete and my burlap sack and head to the plantation. By this time, it's about four in the afternoon. I'm exhausted from the ordeal at school. I pick coconuts until late in the evening, sometimes seven or eight at night.

I'm being lazy. Sometimes I do not go to certain coconut trees to pick the coconuts because I'm afraid of being in the woods and all the strange noises. When my father checks a certain tree the next day and finds coconuts, he gets really mad at me and beats me for not checking that coconut tree.

He doesn't spank me; he beats me hard. So I make sure that, even though I do not want to do something, I do it. I know the ramifications. I don't remember if my parents were ever so concerned about me not being in school or, for that matter, if they ever made sure I went to school. They never seem concerned about it so I don't go very much.

Eventually the mayor comes to the house to see why I'm not in school, and they tell him that I'm too busy picking coconuts. That's the way of life in the village. One time, the mayor tells my parents that if I'm not in school for a certain period of time, they will face charges. So my parents send me to school. I'm afraid of the teacher. I do not want the teacher to smack me or make me kneel in the sun on top of the stone grater. I make excuses not to go. I tell my mother that I need to go and plant corn or pick certain coconut trees deep in the jungle.

So there I am preparing my machete, making sure it's really sharp. I go to get ready to plant corn. I prepare the site by setting the entire area on fire. At the end of the day, I get home full of smoke and soot, dirty and sweaty. I run to the ocean, jump in, and get cleaned up. After this, I eat rice and beans with fried plantains. This is what we eat when there is no meat or fish. If my mother feels really good, she will make soup of flour with flour ball—it's so good. I go to bed with the salt water still on my skin.

The next day, I go back and plant corn. Dolores is so happy about that, she makes me dinner that day. I don't remember where my father is through all of this. He must have been on one of his trips spending money on women and beer. I do not ask where he is any more. All I know is that he's not around much.

At times, I eat just about anything I come across. I go to hunt for iguanas when I feel like eating some meat, or for deer or wild duck. Sometimes, I have to admit, there are certain aggressive wild monkeys, so I will hunt for them and kill them and eat them.

Monkey is a great delicacy; it is a treat for that day. When we eat monkey, there are no rules. I stoop down and just eat, wildly, stuffing my mouth and trying to talk with my mouth full of meat, the juice dripping down all over my chin and hands. I enjoy eating monkey meat. Do not talk to me while I'm eating monkey! It would be dangerous trying to talk to me. I'm in heaven! None of the other kids touch that meat. I don't care! I want to eat something other than rice and beans.

Some of the other kids from the village and I go looking for monkeys, but not just any monkeys, a particular type of monkey. I get really wild when I go to hunt. I transform into an animal, trying to think like an animal, act like an animal. I wear nothing but a leaf to hide my private area. First I cover my entire body with thick mud so the mosquitoes won't bother me while I'm in hunting mode. Then, I paint my face black using the bark from a certain tree. I take a bunch of leaves from another tree, rub them on my hands to make a green color and put it on my face. I go and find another type of tree and make another color, so by the time I'm finished, I look like blend between a tropical bird and a warrior prepared for battle.

I go to the water's edge and try to see my reflection. I'm very scary. I'm satisfied with my appearance. I grab my machete and put it between my teeth. I climb a tree and stoop down very quietly, still with my machete in my mouth. The only things you see of me are my eyes, very small. You would really have to be looking hard to see me stooped in the treetop. I blend in really well so the monkeys do not see me. The other kids are hiding in the bushes quietly, waiting for me to jump after a monkey.

We spend hours preparing ourselves. It is worthwhile. We have a fire going, burning green leaves so that only smoke is coming out of the fire so the mosquitoes don't bother us. We bathe in the smoke, so we smell like smoke. It's wild. After we get a monkey or two, we roast them over the fire and eat them. Then we go and hunt for another one to take home.

We get home carrying monkeys, each one of us, and start taking the skin off. We are full of blood from skinning our kill. Sitting around the table, eating monkey. These are good times.

I spend most of my time wishing I were in some other part of the world. I know that's not going to happen. I also know that I will never get out of this village. I prepare myself to spend the rest of my life here. I keep telling my mother that I'm going to run away every time we fight. We have major disagreements, in part because I'm miserable and I'm mad at myself all the time. I go and chop wood for hours and hours just to relieve some of the tension within me.

If I'm not cutting wood, I'm climbing coconut trees and sitting at the very top, looking at the horizon and going on a trip in my mind. From the top of the coconut trees, I can see jets with the white stream of vapor coming from behind. I wonder where that jet is going. *How can I put myself inside that jet?* I stoop on the top of a coconut branch and make myself really comfortable, as much as possible, and just watch the sky or watch the ocean on the horizon.

From the top of the coconut tree, I also see people passing by from time to time. No one knows that I'm on top of the trees watching. It gives me a sense of comfort, a sense of peace. I'm by myself, enjoying the peace and tranquility of being away from my regular life, hour after hour. It's really great to be there on top. I do not want to come down. I see the jets go by once a day. They seem so close I think I can touch them, but they're miles and miles high. Sometimes I make myself very comfortable and cozy on a branch, lean against the tree trunk, and fall asleep. The ants bite me, but I do not care. I sometimes don't feel the bugs biting me. I see them walking on my arms and know they are on my face, but I feel nothing. I just continue to sleep. My skin is very tough. My feet have so many calluses on the bottoms that I can go up a sixty-foot coconut tree very fast.

My mother never bothers me; she doesn't know that I'm in treetops. The tree sways very gently from the light wind that's blowing and I sway with it, wondering what it would be like to be in another place, if one even exists. I know there is a land that is called the United States, but I do not know where it is on a map. We don't have any maps to see the world. We never see people from the outside world in this village. We just hear of different lands that exist by listening to Radio Belize. It gives us the names of other places. In the afternoons, we hear who has died and the names of the family members of the deceased. They announce the obituaries on the radio and, they announce family member deaths.

Coming down from a coconut tree is very easy. I just hug the tree, align my foot downward, and distance my body from the tree so I'm still holding on with my hands and arms, but not hugging it. All I'm touching with my feet and hands is the tree trunk, and I make sure I stay in a straight line once I'm on the way down. At such a fast rate of speed, if I don't I can lose control and die. I have seen a few close friends die from coming down a coconut tree. I learned the hard way, by practicing my own style of climbing and my own style of coming down. This works for me. We all have different techniques, because the weight of the individual plays a big part in the technique.

You slide down and in a matter of seconds you are down from a sixty-foot tree. When you're on your way down, you need to be prepared to stop the downward motion. Once you get to ground, if you don't have a plan you can get hurt because of the jolt from the speed with which you're coming down. Once you start the downward motion, do not try to stop. You can't stop! If you decide that you're going too fast and you want to slow down, you'll fall off the tree.

When we go and hunt for iguanas and see one on top of a coconut tree, we first make sure it is an iguana, not a snake. We then position dogs three feet away from the tree, making sure the dogs are looking up. The dogs are trained to run and kill animals and they can smell an iguana.

Once the dogs are in position, I climb the tree very slowly from the opposite side of the iguana. I stop midway and look down at the dogs. If they are still in place, I continue climbing until I get to the top. When I reach a coconut branch, I grab it and slowly, quietly, slide down to the tip and surprise the iguana. I startle it, and it jumps to the ground where the dogs are waiting for it.

When iguanas jump from the trees, whether from high or low, they spread their legs. The back legs become like a parachute, and when they land, they land at dead stop. The iguana looks around for a second or two and then it runs. It runs fast. The dogs corner the iguana and the barking tells us where the iguana is located. Once the dogs have the iguana cornered, it can't go anywhere. I slide down the tree, run toward the barking, and grab the iguana by the back of its neck.

I take one of the back legs toward the back body and then front leg toward and I break the two little toes, interlocking both broken toes inside the skin. Then I do the same with the other two legs. The iguana is helpless. I climb the coconut tree again and look for the iguana eggs. We eat them too. Iguana eggs are like caviar; they can be either boiled or eaten raw with lime, salt, and a shot of tequila.

I put the iguana on my shoulders and walk home with dinner. Iguana for dinner! I fry the meat or put it in stew or soup. You have to be very careful when you eat an iguana because it has lots of bones. If you swallow an iguana bone, it can get lodged in your throat; if you swallow it, it can cut your stomach. The bones are so fine, finer than the bones from fish, that they can cause major internal damage.

You always reward the dogs with their share of the meat. You only have enough meat for one meal, so then you go and do the same thing the next day ... or you go fishing.

One time, some of the fishermen from the village go fishing. They leave very early in the morning. They go deep-sea fishing and at about noontime word comes to the people of the village that some of the fishermen have caught a huge whale. My father gets in his small boat along with some other men from the village. They go to see this great whale. Before you know it, dozens of men are trying to capture this huge whale, about fifty fishermen. They finally catch it, and some of them get on top of the whale while it is dragged to shore. We all help by chopping the whale with axes, machetes, or whatever cutting tools we can get our hands on. We all have a hand in it.

I think it takes a whole night to cut up this whale. The head is as big as a plane. We have never seen anything like it! We kids get inside the mouth of the whale and play hide and seek while the entire village is cutting up this huge whale.

There are huge walls of meat. We don't know what to do with all the meat. We eat it for months. We have almost fifty drums of whale oil to cook with for a very long time. We salt the meat and lay it in the sun for days until it is dried. Then we cut sections from it and eat it raw. There is a process it goes through while it is drying. It gets full of maggots. We can see the really big maggots all over the meat, so we clean it well before cooking the meat. The process gives it extra flavor. It takes away the taste of fish and the taste of the ocean. We eat whale meat for breakfast, lunch, and dinner.

I'm not sure of the origin of the coconut. I don't think anyone knows its origin. All I know is that it's a large fruit and it has two extremely hard shells—the outer shell, which is green and the inner shell, which is brown. You can drop a coconut from a ten-story building and I'm sure it will not break—the shell is that tough. But don't take my word for it; I have never tested that theory.

Coconut trees grow near the ocean because they have to have salt water. Without it, the coconuts will not grow. Throughout Latin America, Central America, South America, or the East Indies coconut plantations are located either right on the beach or near the beach, close to the ocean. Coconut trees are more productive when they are near salt water. If a coconut tree is away from the salty waters of the Atlantic, it will grow well and fast, but it will not produce good coconuts, and it will die in a few years.

The coconut has many uses, but the main use is food. Inside the coconut there is liquid to keep the inner white core moist. When the Americas were discovered, the travelers used to seek out coconuts as a food source. It is good and it fills you up. It has many other uses as well.

The white flesh of the fruit is the meat. The center contains a watery liquid that is often sipped straight from the coconut. Coconut milk is made by simmering equal parts water and shredded coconut meat. The meat is strained out and the thick liquid that remains is the milk. Coconut cream is made the same as coconut milk but with a greater proportion of coconut to water (four to one.)

We also collect the coconut's water and make cider by boiling it or we put the coconut water in a drum and seal it for days. The coconut ferments and becomes liquor, ready to drink.

The coconut tree, which lives for a very long time—the life expectancy is fifty or more years—produces thousands of coconuts. The tree never stops producing coconuts in its lifetime. Having thousands of coconut trees with each tree producing constantly can yield a million coconuts in a month's time.

Fresh coconut is available year-round, but October through December is peak season. Just grab the coconut and shake it to see if it has water in it. With most coconuts, you can shake them and listen for a sloshing sound. If you hear water it is a good coconut, it is not dry inside. If you hear that it hardly has any water inside, it may be drying up. The white section is going to have a slimy film on it if it's getting rotten. If that's the case, it will not last long.

It's not easy to open a coconut. The hard shell can't be penetrated without a heavy, sharp knife or a machete. We used to use a pointy iron bar or a tire iron. The bar has to have an angle on the point. We would grab the coconut and, with blunt force, hit the coconut with the sharp point. At this point, the coconut is stuck on the sharp iron point. Then we would take the coconut and push it to one side, hard. One of the sides of the hard shell peels off. Then we would take the other side of the coconut and do the same thing. Next we would grab the coconut and peel the remaining hard shell with our hands. This is only the first step in peeling a coconut.

The next step in peeling a coconut is dealing with the second hard, brown shell. If you want to break through this, it can't just be hit it against a hard object. A coconut can be thrown around as hard as possible and it won't break. We take and hold the coconut with the palms of our hands and bring the coconut down hard once or twice onto the backside of a machete. It then splits in half, exposing the white section of the coconut, which we call the meat.

Being that we have hundreds of coconuts to peel, it can take all day to peel five hundred coconuts. It's tiring, and it takes lots of physical effort and hard labor. We take the outer shells and pile them up in one location near us. At the end of the day, during the evening, we set the pile on fire to make a huge bonfire. All the kids come and play around the fire. Some of the villagers take advantage of the fire to do their cooking for the next day.

There are two or three types of coconut plants. Japanese trees are more of a decoration around homes because they grow small and they look neater. They have either yellow or green shiny coconuts. They are famous because they don't make as much of a mess as wild coconut trees. They can be manicured depending on how the individual wants it to appear around the yard. They typically don't grow more than ten to twenty feet high, while the wild coconut tree can grow from twenty to sixty feet high.

If a tree is sixty feet high, it doesn't produce as many coconuts as a smaller tree. I don't know the reason for this, but if a coconut tree is sixty feet high, you can see that it doesn't produce coconuts. It has just kept growing out of control. Trees like that are cut down and the trunk is used to build homes, or as stilts to lift homes above ground.

Most of my time is spent on the plantation, picking coconuts or sometimes pretending to pick coconuts. But I know that if I do not go and pick certain plants, I will get a beating from my father. He sends me to areas I'm afraid to go to because it is very thick jungle. Very thick! It's so hot and there's no air.

The plantation line is near a huge cemetery. I hate to go around that area because I have heard that bad things happen to people when they go by there. I am so afraid of cemeteries. I am afraid of seeing spirits. So, I hate to go by there, but my father always sends me there the early evening or late afternoon. I am always looking behind me and all around. When I hear a noise, my heart starts pounding. I stop what I'm doing and look hard to see who is there. If I keep hearing the same noise, I just drop what I'm doing and run. I wait a while, and then I go back again later.

I hate going by myself to the jungle, but I have to do it. If I don't, I get beaten either by my mother or my father. And, it's not just a spanking. Forget it! It is a really serious beating. They pull my pants down and I hear that leather belt coming out of my father's pant loops, boy, I almost see smoke coming out of that thing. Then he wraps it around his hand and I hear music when it hits my tender young skin. It hurts so badly!

So, I know better and I pick coconuts where he tells me to, even if I'm scared. I talk loudly to myself and smoke a huge cigar that makes lots of smoke because it's made from grass. According to legend, smoke scares the spirits away.

There I am picking coconuts and talking loudly to myself so I won't get scared (or to scare the spirits away.) Sometimes I answer myself. The cigar smoke makes me look like a chimney, but it serves two purposes; one is to scare the spirits, and the other is to keep the mosquitoes away. At any given time, especially when it rains, a big dark cloud can appear out of nowhere. It's a mass of mosquitoes to chase me! But the smoke keeps them at a distance. I talk about anything that comes into my mind and curse the living daylights out of myself for being born in a bad time or to a bad family. I carry a small plastic bottle of moonshine that helps me forget about my life, and I cannot feel the mosquitoes that do bite me.

When I cut brush, the machete slips and I get cut. I laugh uncontrollably watching the blood pour out. I think nothing of it. I think it's funny because I am drunk and I go home bleeding.

My life is boring, nothing to look forward to; the same thing day after day. My father never does anything to change that.

At Christmastime it rains, but some days are sunny and the evenings are damp. One of the villagers goes around the entire town with a noisemaker, day and night. That man never sleeps. I can hear the loud noisemaker coming from a distance. He comes around our house in the evening to scare the spirits.

Another man who is painted with thick ashes all over his body so no one can recognize him goes and hides himself around the village. He looks so mean and menacing. In the evening, he goes around the town scaring the kids if they do not give him money or some moonshine to drink. When I see him, I go and hide under the bed. That day, I do not go and pick coconuts, but my mother tries to insist that I go. Instead I go hide under the bed, so that the man will not get me. I'm so afraid of him. I'm afraid that he will hurt me because I refuse to give him something.

Whenever we are going to get heavy storms, the ocean gets so calm it almost looks like a sheet of glass—not a wave or a ripple on the water, no wind, very calm. That is how we know there is a storm coming. We also listen to the weather forecast from Belize. Then, sometime in the middle of the night, I can hear the wind whistling outside, the water beating against the house. We keep our fingers crossed hoping that the storm will not wash the house away.

In the morning, we can see the ocean under the house. The house sways from time to time, as if it were on rollers. It's difficult, and I'm afraid when I see the high waves coming toward us, one after the other. We can see the coconut trees swaying and being blown away, or being washed under the house. It's scary.

Sometimes when we are going to have a heavy hurricane, my father will send us to higher ground. He stays behind and looks after the plantation. The water gets so high the plantation becomes flooded and it takes months to dry out. This is when most of the mosquitoes appear.

A few times, I stay behind with my father during hurricanes. All he gives me to eat is canned sardines in oil. Talk about the worst food I have ever eaten! I get so sick at night, and he doesn't do anything to help me or even come to see what the problem is.

Rio Tinto is a very lonely place to live. There is nothing to do in the village. It is full of sand because it's close to the beach. What you see today, you will see tomorrow. Nothing new, every day is the same. You can walk from one end of town to the north the river is, all in about ten minutes and you cannot go any further.

You see the same people every day, doing the same thing every day. They try to do it a bit different, just to do something different. You see most of the men along the beach, napping in hammocks in the shade of the coconut trees. They sometimes go fishing, just to pass the time and for something to eat. Some of them build canoes out of mahogany or other types of wood, but the main tree is mahogany. It's heavy and strong. Some of the men are building fishing nets. They are so fast building huge fishing nets. They are all lined up along the beach under the coconut trees in the early afternoon until late the evening building their fishing nets. These nets are very large, about fifty to one hundred feet long.

Some of the men are building a net they call a *taraya*. It is a circular net with weights along the outer edge. At first when I try to build one, it takes me months to learn the correct technique. But after that, I can build one in a week. It has to be very round and have the right amount of weights around the edges. Then when I go to throw it in the water, I can't do it because it's too heavy for me. But then, after about a year of practice, it becomes very easy for me.

That is how we catch sardines. Every evening, at about six, most of the men line up along the riverbank throwing the *taraya*, catching sardines. Sometimes just one throw will catch hundreds of sardines. We eat some of them made into a soup, and the rest are used for bait.

One night when the moon is full, since one of the villagers and I cannot catch anything in the sea, my father sends us to catch sardines in the river—fresh water sardines. There we are, along the river's edge, throwing the *taraya* late into the night. We come home with buckets of sardines, and we separate them: half for eating and half for deep-sea fishing.

One of the villagers and I, get up at midnight to get started to go fishing with our sardines as bait. We go about a hundred miles out to sea. We spend all the next day in the open ocean, fishing. Two are in a small canoe, one at the back and the other in the front. We are so far away we do not see land. We are fishing for big game fish.

I've gone with my father fishing once or twice, but he does not like taking me with him. He wants me to stay home and pick coconuts. Sometimes he comes home empty-handed. We eat rice and beans then. It's a bad-fishing day that day, and my mother is anticipating my father bringing home fish, so when he comes home with nothing, it's a sad day. This means we have only rice, beans, and plantains. It gets old fast, eating rice and beans and boiled bananas every day, or coconut soup to change the menu.

The women in the village go to the jungle and look for cassava roots and bring them home to make cassava bread. It takes them all day to make that bread. The women in the village are very dedicated to making the bread. Mothers and daughters work together. My mother never makes cassava bread, and the women in the village ask her why she never tries making it. My mother makes bread from flour. It's good, and she sells some of it just to get money to buy sugar or cigarettes.

My mother likes smoking, she is a heavy smoker, and I am too. I smoke two packs of cigarettes a day. I smoke cigarettes and chew tobacco. My mouth is sometimes so full of tobacco that I cannot talk. I stuff in as much as I can. I also smoke a pipe. I take the large claw of a blue crab and split it in half to make a pipe. The smell is so bad, it's crazy. I also smoke big cigars. I make my own cigars from dry grass or bark from the trees. I smoke heavily or I build a fire pit to bathe in the smoke when I am picking coconuts so I smell like smoke so the mosquitoes do not bite me. I build the fire and then put lots of green leaves from any tree in the fire. I take my shirt off and walk around in the heavy smoke. I lean against a coconut tree, holding my breath. I spend hours doing this trick, and from the house the heavy smoke can be seen up in the air.

I look for a special green leaf and rub it with my hands and spread it all over my face. I cut a wild bush that grows along the beach to collect the milky substance it produces which I spread all over my body. This way, when the mosquitoes attack me they never penetrate the skin. They get stuck in the milky substance. I walk around the plantation with no shirt, but I cannot feel the mosquitoes at all.

Here I am with a green face, no shirt, smoking a huge cigar, and sometimes half drunk. I'm walking on air, never feeling anything. I'm talking to myself and laughing out loud. This is simply a part of my life, my lonely and depressing life. Every day is the same. Why not be stupid and do crazy things to entertain myself?

Sometimes tarantulas walk on top of my head without me knowing it until I feel the legs slowly crawling down forehead. I laugh at it and call it my friend and give it a kiss. I'm just trying to explore my manhood, even though I know that I'm still a long, long way from it. I'm just a little boy who can't even fish.

The next time I ask Samantha, a young native girl, for a hug and a kiss on the lips, I plan to give her three young coconuts and even take her mother and father a dozen of the best coconuts that we have. She lives on the plantation and I want to hug her. I even go hunt for a whole white-faced monkey hoping to impress her, just so she will give me a hug, hoping that she says she will.

I find some monkeys deep in the jungle. I catch a mother and her baby, and I take them to Samantha's house and give them to her parents. They accept the gift. But I'm so shy. I'm outside their house looking down the whole time, hoping that Samantha will say yes to the hug.

A few days later, I see her again and she says yes to the hug. At this time, I'm feeling really good. I'm planning my life with her in the village and even asking my mother to have a piece of the property so I can live there when they leave. I plan to have some of the villagers help me build a hut out of coconut fronds, and I plan to give them corn soup in return. I'm also starting a cornfield near where I want to live. I know that I'm still a boy, but I'm going to end up in that village for the rest of my life. I guess I'm preparing myself for the worst. Just me, Samantha, the jungle, the plantation, the sea, and the bright blue sky.

I still dream though. I go to the plantation near the cemetery, lean against a tree, and look at the sky, watch the planes pass by, hope someday something good will happen. I wish I were inside one of those planes going by going to wherever that plane might take me.

Sometimes I cry and hate myself, curse God for my life. I curse at Him, asking why he made me come into this miserable world in Rio Tinto. I have rotten teeth (I never brush my teeth), hardly take a bath, and what do I know about anything? Sometimes I sob and sob, asking myself, *Why?* I kneel on the hot sand; ask God, *Why couldn't I have been like the normal boys in the world. What did I do, or what did my parents do to have me?* Born in this miserable place no one knows anything about; the world doesn't even know that we exist. If the government doesn't know we exist, then no one knows. We're not even on the map. If someone wants to find us, there is only one way in and one way out of this forgotten place.

I see big cargo ships go by at all hours of the day and night. I don't think they even know that there are people living here in these small villages. At night, there are no lights. It is pitch dark. The only light we have is from candles or kerosene lanterns. The people who have money, people that have been in the States, they send money to their relatives. They have flashlights in their houses. When they walk around, they carry their flashlights.

I am a jungle boy. I will always be a jungle boy. I'm mean, I'm tough, I'm angry; don't mess with me because I will do you harm.

We have heard that there is a thing called a refrigerator that keeps food cold, or you can make things that freeze called popsicles. We have not seen one of them yet. We have also heard that there's a machine that cuts grass called a lawnmower. We have not seen one of those either. I'm sure we can use one of them here at the house to cut grass. We have also heard that there is a thing that shows moving pictures for entertainment, and you can see people moving in pictures right in front of you on a screen. I think it would be fun to see people moving on a screen for entertainment.

One day, the government sends a group of people from the city to show the moving pictures to us in the village. We all gather inside the schoolhouse. They have a generator with them. There we are packed like sardines inside the tiny schoolhouse waiting for the moving picture to start. There are no chairs so we are all standing up. We are all happy because we're going to see a moving picture, with people in it, on a white sheet. It's very hot that evening around eight. We wait for about an hour while the city people are trying to work out how to make the moving picture work.

We are all holding candles to light the room. Finally they tell us to blow the candles out because the moving picture is about to start. Here we are, all of us holding our breath. We are about to see a moving picture for the first time. This is such a big deal! I want to see people light up doing tricks in front of me on that white sheet.

Finally after a while, the moving picture starts. We are totally surprised to see people moving in pictures in front of us, walking in the lights on white sheet. Everyone in the room is so surprised that they scream. Everyone is screaming so loud because we think that the moving picture is coming out of the wall. We are amazed to see a light bring people to life. We look at the machine that is showing the moving picture. We think it is black magic.

This is something that we have never seen before so when we see people jumping from a high building, we all scream. We think that the people on the screen are coming toward us so we back away. Some run out of the schoolhouse, most of us are afraid.

I stand in front of the light coming out of the machine to see what's making the picture move. I put my hands in front of it. I touch the light then the machine. I'm very curious and I'm also scared. I think that the action is happening outside, so I run there to look for the building that the man on the sheet is jumping from. I do not know what is happening. I think it's real, so I go back inside to see it again. The people inside are still screaming, "Black magic!"

I think I must be dreaming or that it really is black magic. It is an amazing scene at the schoolhouse that night, watching magic before us. It was breathtaking!

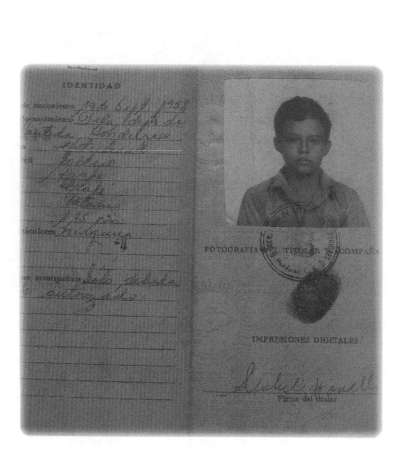

CHAPTER 6

The Beatings

From time to time, we get into these coughing fits. When one starts to cough, we all start to cough. The temperature can go as low as fifty-five degrees in the evenings. We wear no shoes, sometimes no cloths, so we walk around in the nude, and we get colds. Sometimes we start to cough in the evenings while we're in bed. One night I can't stop coughing. So Dolores makes me drink castor oil or fish oil. And I hate it! It's the worst thing to drink. First comes the smell and as you start to swallow it, it just goes down so slowly. Even if you put salt or lemon juice in it, it is still awful and that doesn't take the smell away. It does stop the coughing though.

If we know we are going to be coughing we stuff our bed sheets in our mouths so Dolores and Sealie won't hear us. I'm one of the biggest coughers around, I think. Once I start to cough, I cannot stop coughing, even if I put sheets over my mouth.

One night I'm coughing and coughing some more. I cannot stop, so Dolores pulls me out of bed and drags me to the kitchen and makes me drink the oil. I don't know if you've ever smelled castor oil or fish oil, or if you've had to drink it, but I hate it! I watch her take out the wooden spoon, open the bottle of fish oil, pour the oil in the spoon, and put it near my mouth. I hesitate and grab her hand, but she pushes it toward me more. I grab her hand hard. I start crying so that she won't make me drink it, but she insists. She says, "If you do not take this, I will spank you."

I cry more and beg her not to make me drink the oil. This is an ongoing thing in the evenings when we have colds. I feel sick from coughing and afraid of the taste of the oil. My brother and sisters cough too, and she makes them drink fish oil, and they, too, cry and resist her.

I am around six years old at this time, I think. I'm afraid of Sealie and my mother. They seem so harmless to everyone else, but believe me . . . So, one night I remember going to bed, wrapping myself in the sheets so that only my nose is sticking out in order to breathe. I make sure that I put a big piece of the sheet in my mouth so that if I were to cough, they would not hear me. This particular night, I start to cough repeatedly. I cannot stop, and they hear me. Dolores jumps from her bed, pulls me out of my bed, drags me to the kitchen, and tries to make me drink the fish oil.

I refuse to drink it, so she beats me up very badly. She then puts me outside the house, closes the door, and locks it. It's dark outside, around midnight. I'm so scared of the dark and I'm crying my eyes out, begging her to open the door and promising her that I will drink the fish oil. After an hour or so, I finally see a light in the kitchen and she is opening the door. She lets me in and hands me a spoon of fish oil. Again, I hesitate, so she beats me up again. What a beating! She puts me outside again, this time for the night.

I survive that night; I don't know how, but I do. The next day she sends me to pick a branch of a tree, not too thin or too thick so she can beat me with it at night whenever I do not want to drink the fish oil.

When I'm sick, it seems I only cough in the evenings, or at night and not during the day. It is around one in the morning. I'm coughing and again, I'm pulled out of bed to be given the fish oil. This time Sealie is the one giving it to me! I hesitate, I can't help it. I wet myself because I know that he is not going to take "no" for an answer. I take the foul stuff in my mouth, and while I think he is not looking, I spit it out. He turns around and sees it. I'm not quick enough. He gets mad, and he pours another spoonful, this time bigger.

I start crying and do not want to drink it, so he puts me outside of the house in the dark again. I'm crying, as usual, and after a short time I promise I will drink the darn oil. He opens the door, and he hands me two spoonfuls. I refuse to take it, so he goes to his room and gets a belt. He does not have to tell me what he is going to do, I already know.

He picks me up by my hair and, holds me in the air, and starts whipping me with the belt. I'm crying and screaming and I think he is never going to stop. Dolores does not come to the rescue; she never comes to help me. Everybody hears, but does nothing.

Sealie opens the door and throws me down the steps. Remember, there are ten to fifteen stairs. He runs down and beats me some more. He picks me up and throws me in the air. He catches me in mid-air and then throws me in the shed with the chickens. The shed is full of tin cans, some are empty and some are filled with kerosene. All I know is that I'm being thrown around like a paper doll. How he is able to see me in the dark is beyond me. The chickens are making clucking in panic, the dogs are howling, and I'm being given the beating of a lifetime.

Finally, after I-don't-know-how-long, it's over, and he leaves me lying amidst tin cans and chickens until the next morning, when Dolores comes to look for me. I'm black and blue and I cannot move. My body is so sore. Sealie wants me to go pick coconuts.

I drag myself out of the shed and get a bit cleaned up and grab my machete and go to pick coconuts. I'm deathly afraid of Sealie from that point on. I'm even afraid to talk to him. If I do not do what he tells me to do, he beats me. This goes on for a long time, with the other kids too. Not as much with them as with me because I'm the only one who goes to pick coconuts. Dolores does nothing to intervene. She's being beaten all the time too. Now when I pick coconuts, I'm full of hatred toward Sealie. I fixate and meditate on everything I'm going to do to him if I ever have my chance. All sorts of hateful thoughts come to my mind. I'm tired of living in this jungle, this wilderness, when he has so much money. He never buys us anything, not even a pair of shoes for me to wear in the jungle while I'm picking coconuts. We have to walk barefoot or sometimes naked because we have no clothes to wear, yet he is rich. I will never forget those beatings. They were horrible.

I am angry now. I carry all of this anger he has created in me. I want to do major damage to him and to anyone who comes my way, I do not care who it is. I want revenge . . . on anyone. So, I start planning . . .

It is a sunny day and we are listening to Radio Belize, the only station Sealie listens to because he only understands English. We listen to Radio Belize because it's more reliable for weather and news from the United States. They are predicting that it's going to be a nice, warm day. I want to go swimming with the rest of the kids, and Dolores approves saying that it would be great to go swimming with the other kids in the village.

The water is beautiful. The ocean is a bit rough but not too bad. Some of the kids in the village have their own little canoe they use to go fishing. Now they use it to have fun. It's not made for adults.

My older sister, Saina, is watching over me. I'm having a great time, the first time I have been swimming in a long time. After a while, I notice that one of the neighbor kids is in his little canoe, running the waves, playing and looking like he's having fun. I go to ask him if I can go with him to run the waves. His canoe is only three feet long, but it's pretty deep. It's solid mahogany, and it must be about two feet deep, enough for two kids to get in and run the waves.

The waves are breaking fast and far. We get in the canoe, the two of us, and start heading to deeper waters. We're having difficulties because the waves keep coming one after the other, really fast. The canoe is taking on water; I try to scoop the water out with my hands, but I can't keep up. We are waiting for the right moment when we see an opportunity to advance between waves. Finally, after waiting a bit, we see that the waves have subsided. We start to paddle faster and faster, and then a huge wave comes and tips us over. I'm disoriented. I do not know where I am. I'm struggling to stay above water, bobbing up and down. I cannot touch the bottom.

Luckily, Saina sees me as I'm trying to stay above water. The waves keep crashing over me. I'm screaming. I do this for what feels like ten minutes, the waves coming one after the other. I can't keep up with them, and I'm screaming at Saina. Finally, I just can't keep up. I'm getting tired of splashing. I'm swallowing seawater. I keep yelling at Saina for help, and I see her yelling at me but I can't hear her. I feel the current taking me under. I swallow more water and go under. I see her jump into the water and start swimming toward me. She reaches me and then I'm out. I do not remember her pulling me out of the water.

The next thing I know, I'm lying on the shore, and Saina is beating on my chest and all this water pouring out of me. I'm coughing so hard I cannot catch my breath. We walk home. We live only about a thousand feet away from the ocean.

Later that afternoon, Sealie comes home from picking coconuts. He looks sweaty and tired. He looks like he had a bad day. Saina tells him what happened that afternoon. I'm standing there, looking down, and starting to feel angry. I'm listening to her telling him the whole story. She is speaking in Spanish, but he does not understand

Spanish, so I'm hoping that he does not understand her. I'm still looking down.

I hear him pulling the leather belt out of his belt loops. He pulls it out so fast. I hear the belt as it makes its way out of each slot. Thwack, thwack, thwack. It should be smoking it comes out so fast. I watch him pull it out; I stand there frozen. Time seems to slow as the belt makes its way out of each individual loop. It's smoking hot. He wraps it around his hand. I'm prepared for this. I'm counting the seconds it takes to reach my skin. Oh boy! By the time it gets to me, I have prepared myself for it. I watch him wrap it around one hand, making a fist as he is getting ready to swing it. He grabs me by my hands and starts to swing. I see the belt make contact before I feel it. It hurts badly! I know that with him I cannot grab ahold of the belt because it will be worse, much worse. He still has me by the hands and now lifts me up in the air. He keeps swinging until he is satisfied. Finally, he throws me to the ground, another bad day.

He says, "Go pick coconuts!"

I'm on the ground, unable to move as fast as he wants. I'm in pain and struggle to get up. I'm pushing myself up slowly, crying hard, my clothes full of dirt, a dirty face, and mud on my elbows. He extends his foot under my body and pulls me up with a hard kick. I am still hoping that my mother will do something to help me, but she just watches my agony.

It's just another day at the Lowell house, to say the least. I'm in pain all the rest of the day and into the night. My ribs are so sore I can hardly move. In bed, I sleep facing up without moving.

The next day, he and I walk to the river as if nothing ever happened, not saying anything. We get to the riverbank, and there he grabs me by my shirt collar and pulls me up in the air again. I don't know what's happening. He throws me in the river, and he says, "Swim! Swim!"

The river has a slow current, and there I am splashing, swallowing the mucky water. He stands there and keeps watching me splash as the current is dragging me toward the ocean. This part of the river is where the river runs into the ocean. I do not want to call for help but I'm terrified. At last he jumps in the water, grabs me, and pulls me out. He yells, "I told you to swim!"

I am in the sand trying to catch my breath. I'm panting and coughing, breathing very fast. I'm lying in the sand, and he puts one foot up and steps on my chest. He pulls me up from the beach and lifts me onto the horse, bareback. He slaps the horse's buttocks, and the horse takes off running.

I'm still coughing and I cannot control the horse because it has no harness or rope. I'm gripping the horse's mane. The horse is running out of control. He is spooked. Eventually, I don't know how, but the horse makes it home. He comes to a stop at the bottom of the steps of our house. I'm wet, tired, and scared. I slide off and go in the house.

The following afternoon, just when I think this ordeal is over, Sealie drags me to the river again. I'm petrified; I don't know what he is going to do this time. He puts two fifty-five gallon drums together and ties them together with rope. He throws them in the water, lifts me up, and puts me in between the two drums. He drags the drums to the middle of the river with me in the middle. He watches me from the shoreline as the current is dragging me out to sea again. I'm splashing, but this time I'm not swallowing any water. I'm letting the current drag me, and I think to myself, *this is different*. When I get to the ocean, he gets in his canoe and paddles toward me. He throws me a rope, I grab the rope, and he pulls me to shore. I'm a bit relieved, because he does not beat me this time. He stoops down and he looks at me, I don't look at him.

Sealie is getting sicker by the day. Every time he gets pain in his back, behind his ribs, he has to lean backwards. Dolores presses a drinking glass against his skin and that seems to relieve the pain for a while. Sometimes she has to put a copper penny inside the glass, put it against his skin, and leave it there for about five minutes. Sometimes we make medicine from roots or grass and that seems to help calm the pain.

These are the old-world remedies. Whenever the machete cuts us, we stop the bleeding by burning a cloth and rubbing the ashes in our hands so the ashes become very fine. Then we sprinkle the dust in the wound and close the wound by wrapping it and letting it heal. That stops the bleeding.

Ernest and Prudence leave Rio Tinto to go to the island Utila for a few days, so Sealie watches their house. I go and keep Sealie company in the evenings.

One evening, it's raining hard and there's lightning and thunder. Late that night, Sealie starts to experience pain again. I go to his bedside and try to comfort him. I'm worried because I don't know what to do. I sit and talk to him. I ask if he wants me to go home and bring Dolores, but he says no.

I pace to the front door and back to the bedroom, trying to figure out what to do. Sealie is screaming from the pain. I feel the tears burning my eyes as I walk back and forth from the door and back and then the length of the bedroom. I listen, then stop and look in on him as he suffers. I feel so dumb, as if I cannot do anything for him. He's in pain; and I cannot help him. All I do is pace, up and down, biting my fingernails, trying to figure out what to do, crying, hoping that his pain will stop. The lightning and thunder outside do not relent. I can hear the rain pounding. I'm very afraid of the dark, but I decide to run home and tell Dolores to come over to see Sealie.

I open the door and look outside. I cannot see anything but darkness, the rain, and occasionally the bright lightning that lights up some of the house. I stand in the doorway listening to Sealie moan from the pain for a moment then I make a run for it to go get Dolores. I run through the middle of the coconut plantation because if I were to go through the middle of town the dogs would eat me up. It's raining hard. I run as fast as I can and trip over a fallen coconut tree that is blocking the darkened dirt pathway. I fall in a deep puddle of water and become disoriented. I don't know where I am. I try to get up, crying and begging God to help me see the way. I'm soaking wet. Lightning and thunder strike. I look up and can see where I am! I get up. Blood is gushing from the cuts on my legs, but I start running again anyway. The lightning lasts just long enough for me to see where I'm.

I begin to limp, not able to run any longer, I crawl home. I get home and I am not able to speak. I am frightened, cold, wet, bleeding, and I have just run almost five miles. Dolores gets herself ready and starts walking with me back to see Sealie. When we arrive, Dolores comforts him to sleep. With no doctors or medicine in the small village, he has to endure the pain.

Sealie has always said that if something were to happen to him, not to take him to his in-laws', Dolores' parents' house for the funeral. He stresses that again to Dolores. He doesn't like the in-laws because they never approved of him marrying Dolores.

Dolores arranges for Sealie to be taken away to a hospital a few days later. She pays a few men from village to take him to the river where they have a small canoe with a six-horsepower motor. That evening, around nine, the four men get to the house and put Sealie in a fabric stretcher, and carry him to the river. The four men make their way with my father through the plantation using flashlights to light the way. Dolores follows them. I stay home with the younger kids. Carmela and Saina go with Dolores.

They get Sealie to the canoe, and they take him to the nearest train station fifty miles up river. They arrive at about two in the morning. Dolores goes knocking at different homes to see if someone will let them in for a few hours. At one of the households, someone recognizes her and lets them in.

Around eight o'clock the next morning the morning, the train pulls into the station, and they board the train heading to San Pedro Sula. They admit Sealie to the hospital, Francisco Morazán Medical Center.

I stay home with Janelle, George, and Jacinta. I take care of them for a few weeks while Dolores is with Sealie. I get up in the morning and make breakfast for them and then head for the plantation to pick coconuts. I'm taking care of one-hundred-and-fifty acres of plantation all by myself. Afterwards, I come home and cook for my younger brother and sisters. I'm only seven years old.

After a few weeks, Dolores comes back to see us, but a week later she goes back to the city leaving us once again. I'm lonely and sad to see Dolores go again, leaving me alone to care for the others. I go and hunt for iguanas to eat. I bring the kill home, skin it and cook it. The others do not like what I make or how I cook. I put the kill on a stick over the fire and serve it with plantains. That's dinner.

Since I am afraid of the dark, the evenings and nights are very difficult for me. Now I have to take care of the other kids. We sit on the steps that overlook the town, alone, just us, looking into a lonely town of Rio Tinto with nothing around, nothing interesting to see, only jungle. I sit with Jacinta on my lap, feeling rather sad, not knowing when Dolores is going to come back. It has been more than two weeks since she left. Life seems so hard, lonely, and unpredictable for me at this time.

Dolores has been gone for two months now, and I'm in the plantation picking coconuts, my face is full of sweat, I'm wearing a dirty shirt, and no shoes. I'm chopping brush. I get home that day to find Dolores there. She tells us the news that Sealie has died. She says she has come to take all of us to the funeral. She tells us that we are going to travel to the city of San Pedro Sula. I'm shocked and sad, I run into the plantation and hide in the brush, crying.

A few hours later, Dolores comes looking for me. She finds me hiding in the brush, crying. I ask her, "What are we going to do, Mama? I'm afraid!" I'm sobbing out of control. Dolores just looks at me very calmly and nods her head as if to say it is going to be okay.

That night, we sleep with the lights on because we're afraid of the dark. I wrap myself up in the blankets with only my nose exposed, afraid that the spirit of Sealie will come and beat me.

The next day, Dolores goes looking for Domain, a local guy who used to work for Sealie. She asks him if he can stay on the property for a few weeks until we come back from the funeral. He agrees, and we leave later that evening.

It's one of the longest trips up the river ever. We leave at six in the evening and do not get to our destination, until midnight. We're all cold, and I stay under the deck of the canoe.

We arrive in the small town called Treinta y Dos. It's a town of farmers. They're bad people. If you look at one of them the wrong way, he'll cut your head off. Their reputation is that they are all mean, the farmers from the interior valleys. They all walk around with machetes strapped around their shoulders, and they all have cuts on their faces, hands, arms, and legs mainly from fighting but some from farming.

We stay in Treinta y Dos that night at a house owned by people Dolores trusts. The next day, we get cleaned up, put on our old shoes and clean shirts, and board the train. It's a cargo train and it stops at every station loading cattle, pigs, chickens, and just about anything that's alive that you can think of. It has almost fifty cars, and every time it gets to a station, we feel the train jerking along as we start to move again.

Many of the people who board look so mean with their guns on their waists and a machetes hanging from their shoulders. Some of them limp from old injuries and some are missing an arm or a leg. It's a sight to see. From the time we board the train to the time we get to San Pedro Sula. It's an all-day event.

It's six in the evening when we pull into the station in San Pedro Sula. We get into a taxi and go to Dolores' parent's house. Carmela and Saina are already here, and now the rest of the family has arrived. Carmela was the only one able to go to the hospital to see Sealie while he was on his deathbed. She is very proud about that, and we, the rest of the kids, feel like outsiders.

Now the adults are trying to figure out how to bring Sealie's body out of the hospital. The hospital does not have an ambulance service so around nine the next evening, Dolores decides to put Sealie's coffin in a taxi. She calls a taxi and it comes to the front of the hospital. They bring the coffin out, and the next thing is trying to figure out how to put a wooden box in a taxi.

We all watch this event taking place. Talk about embarrassment. Here is the taxi driver handling a wooden box, trying to stuff it in the taxi. After a while watching this spectacle, he shoves the wooden box through the back-door window. The wooden box is sticking halfway out of the rear-door window. Then, we all have to fit inside the taxi. So we all squeeze in to the front and back seats. We are driving through the city with a dead man's coffin sticking out of a taxicab's rear-door window. That is the first time that I have seen a coffin in a taxi!

Well, we make it, and they put Sealie's coffin in the living room of Dolores's parents' house. They leave the wooden box open through the night. Talk about freaking out—we cannot sleep. There are so many noises, and I keep hearing people walking. Some of the other kids say that they see things in the dark that are unexplainable. There were lots of unexplained things that night. I wouldn't be surprised if he was trying to let us know of his discontent about being taken to his in-laws' house. We all wake up the next day and go to cry over Sealie's wooden box coffin. We cannot stop looking at his body lying there in the living room.

The living room has two doors, one door facing the street toward the east, and the other door looking onto the porch and the street toward the north. Around two o'clock, Dolores, her mother, and Saina are sitting on the porch talking. The rest of the kids are in the kitchen eating lunch. It's just another day with an open coffin in the living room. The living room doors are wide open when a huge black bird flies into the house from the east door. It flies toward the dining room, toward the kitchen, and over the wooden box. As soon as the bird flies over the wooden box, Sealie's left eye opens! Opens wide! We are all panicked and horrified and do not know what to make of it.

Dolores approaches the wooden box, leans forward, extends her right arm, touches the eye and tries to close the eye, but it will not close. She sends some of us to go downtown to look for a priest. We cannot find a priest. Finally, after a desperate search, we find a Seventh-day Adventist priest, and we tell him what has happened. He looks concerned, and says "Oh! Oh! Praise God!" "My brothers and sisters, the Lord has spoken!" "We need to do a cleansing of the house and of the body.

"Oh shit!" we say. So we bring this priest over and when he sees the eye, he is taken by surprise. "My Jesus! My Jesus! Your body! Oh Lord! He has spoken loud and clear!" He starts asking a bunch of religious questions and telling us what cleansing is all about. He leans forward with caution, we can see him trembling, and with a slight hesitation he extends his right arm, tries to close the eye, but he is not successful. He closes his eyes says "Oh Lord! The body is full of evil! Lord cleanse the body of all of the toxic evil that exists in it!" We are all around the coffin, listening, watching, really scared, and thinking that Sealie has come back from the dead to see where he is.

That evening, around, we take the wooden box to the cemetery in a taxi again. It's such a sight to see, a wooden box riding in a taxi to the cemetery. We pay our last respects with the priest present. Only the family is present at the funeral and there is lots of crying. Dolores faints and I walk around looking sad.

They close coffin lid. I don't know why but the top of the coffin has a small window right over Sealie's face. As they lower the coffin into the ground, we can see the open eye looking at all of us. As they start to shovel the dirt on top of the wooden box, that eye doesn't stop looking at us. Suddenly, as we are all watching, the eye closes! We are all crying and freaking out over what we are seeing. We all think that he was looking to see if he was out of his in-laws' house.

Sealie died at the age of forty-one. There was speculation about the cause of death. No one knows how he died; not even Dolores knows. Some say voodoo killed him, that his in-laws practiced voodoo on him because he stole their daughter from them. Anything is possible.

Dolores notifies Sealie's sister Carmela in the States about the death, but Carmela does not come in time for the funeral. She gets there three days later. We meet her with the help of a family member translating. She cannot speak Spanish.

We are all there, little Carmela, Saina, George, Janelle, Jacinta and I; we are all there, with our aunt Carmela with her blonde hair, high heels, and tight pants. We are all staring at her as she speaks, not knowing what is going on, no knowing what she is saying. We're all grieving the death of Sealie.

She's asking Dolores questions about Rio Tinto and all the property that they have and what is going to happen to it. Aunt Carmela says she wants to sell the property. She is going to find an investor in the States to buy the property. Dolores agrees to sell. Carmen tells Dolores that she is going to send Juney in three weeks to pick us up so he can take us to Utila. Dolores agrees. Carmela says she will pay for the whole trip, about one hundred dollars.

We are watching our aunt speaking in English. We are on our best behavior, on orders from Dolores. She has told us that if we misbehave, we will get spanked. So we are sitting in a circle in the small house of this woman who is from the island of Utila, who is some distant relative of the Lowells. Her name is Dulce but we have never met her before.

Young Carmela is tries to be a show-off. She walks to Aunt Carmela's side and tries to speak English. We're not impressed. The rest of us are sucking on lollipops, making that sucking sound very loudly. Dolores tells us to be quiet.

Dolores is dressed in all black with a white hat. For the first time, we are all clean, wearing something decent. We are so used to being dirty and sweaty, not clean. We feel so strange sitting there, listening to this woman who is making plans for us.

Dolores does not have to worry about money. She has no money. Carmela even asks her if she knows what happened to the money that Ernest and Sealie have. Dolores tells them she does not know what happened to it all. Dolores says that they have lots of cut lumber to build a few houses on the island. Carmela says she is going to tell Juney to bring a barge for the lumber. I'm so excited to hear that we are going to move to Utila.

After about an hour, which seems like an eternity sitting down listening to a woman from the United States, Carmela looks at me and asks if I want to go to Utila to live. I nod my head yes. I am scared, but happy.

We all say good-bye to Carmela and we get into a taxi and go back to Dolores's parents' house. The next day, we get ready to go back to Rio Tinto. Young Carmela, Saina, and I do not want to go back. The train drops us off in the town of Treinta y Dos. Here we get into a small canoe back to Rio Tinto.

It's such a long trip in the middle of the afternoon. It's a hot and muggy day. We are sweating so much that our clothes are wet. We all look so miserable and we are. Dolores has told us on the trip that she is not going to go to Utila. She is not going to listen to that woman from the United States. Whatever Carmela says is nothing but bull, so we'd better not listen. There is not going to be any trip to Utila—we should put it out of our minds. I am extremely disappointed knowing that we are going to end up back in Rio Tinto with no way out.

We get home at about six that evening, and all the villagers are coming one by one to pay their respects. They bring us food and talk about Sealie. Some of the men tell stories about him, and some of them are crying. They tell her if there is anything that they can do, to let them know. They want to help her, especially with the plantation.

We go and tell Ernest that his son was buried and that his daughter Carmela was there. Ernest doesn't seem to be so thrilled about it. He does not seem to be worried or sad. He just goes on with his business, not showing any emotion. At this time, Ernest has no one working for him any more. He stays to himself, always inside the house, staring out the window alone and pathetic. Prudence has gone to the island of Utila to live; she is a sick woman.

Ernest is the only one who has stayed behind to oversee the property.

We try to go on with our lives without Sealie. It's very difficult. Some men in steal my sister Carmela and rape her. It's around five in the evening. Saina is sitting on the porch with Jacinta in her lap and Carmela is sitting on the storefront counter. She is about fourteen. Nando Licona is in the kitchen, talking to Dolores, trying to distract her. Nando Licona calls Saina to the kitchen, and by the time Saina returns to the porch because Jacinta is crying, Carmela is gone.

We all trusted Nando Licona. He was a great friend to us and to Sealie, and so we could not understand why he would betray us. Especially when he was one of the guys who told us that we could trust him for whatever we needed.

We all run out looking for Carmen, but she's nowhere to be found. Finally, Dolores goes and grabs Sealie's gun. She goes outside and starts firing the gun up in the air. She says that if Carmela can't be found, she is going to anyone who looks suspicious.

Finally, Carmela is found with her dress off in back of one of the neighbor's houses. So Dolores goes looking for the guy responsible. Nando tells Dolores it is a neighbor named Geronimo. Dolores is so mad. She is ready to kill the guy. We are all afraid she will.

From that time on, I know that things have changed in the village. I'm so afraid to go to pick coconuts; I always make sure my machete is well sharpened. I look over my shoulder, not trusting anyone. I put traps in different areas of the plantation. I want to kill the people who want to do harm to us. From time to time, I find people in the trap. I then do whatever I want with them, sometimes make them disappear, or drag them to the ocean, or fill the hole with sand.

It has been three weeks since we saw our aunt Carmela. The day comes for us to leave for Utila. I know Dolores has said that we are not going to be going, but I am still hopeful. The morning comes. I have been looking forward to this day with anticipation, hoping that Dolores will change her mind. I watch out of the kitchen window that has a view of the ocean. I'm looking toward Punta Sal, the direction from which Juney's boat will come. After watching for a long time, I see his boat pulling a barge approaching. I know it is Juney! I run to the shore and wait for the boat to get closer. I run home and tell Dolores that Juney is coming and to get ready so we can all go to Utila. She does not seem eager that he is coming.

I now know that we are not going to make the trip. All of my hopes, excitement, dreams, go down the drain. I'm so disappointed and unhappy that day. I feel so cold, as if my life is over. I watch the boat getting closer and closer until Juney's boat drops anchor, and Juney comes to shore.

He sees me and asks if I'm ready to go to Utila. I do not say anything. I think he reads the expression on my face. He asks for Dolores, and I tell him where to find her. We walk together, and I'm hoping that he can talk her into going at the last minute.

As we walk toward the house, we see Dolores sitting on the steps. Juney shakes her hand and asks her if she is ready. He tells her he brought a barge to take the lumber and the family to Utila. Carmela has paid him a lot of money to make this special trip to pick up the Lowell family. Dolores looks at him and says that she and the kids are not going anywhere. Juney asks her if this is her final decision because he cannot spend much time here. He needs to be at another town to pick up coconuts. She sends him away.

I walk with Juney back to his canoe. He gets in and paddles back to his boat. I'm sitting in the sand, staring at the boat. He pulls up the anchor; the engines start. I watch the boat leaving. It's one of the most heartbreaking moments of my life. I think about Juney making the trip for nothing, I'm livid and miserable; I want to tell Dolores off. I walk home crying as I look back from time to time at the Juney's boat fading away into the distance.

I feel the sun has permanently set in my life. All the excitement I had about leaving Rio Tinto has been extinguished. I spend the entire rest of the day crying, sobbing. I do not want to talk to Dolores or to anyone, ever!

The next day, I ask Dolores why we did not go. She says, "This is where we are going to live and die. The sooner you get it through your head, the better off we are going to be, and the better we'll get along."

So I go on picking coconuts, putting traps around the plantation, and being miserable. I hate everybody, especially Dolores, knowing that this is going to be my life. No way out as long I live.

Dolores never tells us that she loves us or gives us any type of affection. I start going out to the plantation to be with the monkeys, trying to get close to them. I spend more time playing with the monkeys than I spend with my brothers and sisters, I do not want be with them. I'm sad, and the monkeys are the best friends I have. We play; they play with me. I eat wild fruits with them.

The terrain is rough, and there are so many mosquitoes. I keep smoking big cigars to keep the mosquitoes away. I look behind me and see a big dark cloud. It's a swarm of mosquitoes coming after me!

I wade through waist-high swamps just to find places where people make moonshine. The swamps are full of animals. My toes feel the way by touching what is underneath them in the mucky black water. There are thorn branches hanging down. The water is full of thorns, leeches, and mosquitoes. I move very slowly along, making sure I don't step down when my feet feel the thorns. There are snakes crawling in the trees and lots of bugs that crawl on my skin, but I do not mind. It's stress relief for me. I come out with leeches stuck on my skin, and I try to get them off. I pick them off with my machete, and sometimes I cut myself.

I find the moonshine shacks and I wait until the people leave. I go and raid their moonshine productions. I start drinking and get drunk out of depression and sadness.

I am a miserable child. I want to kill anyone who would betray us because I know that this needs to be part of my life. We are going to stay in Rio Tinto for a long time; forever. I am getting my mind ready for the unpredictability and monotony of life in the jungle.

I start to not care about anything, about anyone in the village, or for that matter about myself. I only want to rule the jungle. Anyone who comes across me who steals coconuts has to deal with me! I will find methods to hurt them in the worst possible way. I will try to inflict the maximum pain possible.

I am out of control. Since Dolores does not care about me or what I do, I am going to take matters into my own hands. The people in the village know that also—that we, meaning *me*, are going to protect the coconut plantation. I am in the plantation every day checking to see if I can find out who has been stealing from us and I set traps to catch them. When I do, they will have to deal with me. I am not afraid! Actually, I am not afraid of anything any more!

Well, sometimes I am afraid of the spirits, like noises in the bushes, noises that come from nowhere. I think they are ghosts. There are ghosts in this village, and they make themselves visible sometimes. Sometimes I'm in the brush, picking coconuts, and I feel things pulling on my shirt or touching my skin. Sometimes I can see them passing in the dry bush. I run away from wherever I am when it happens, screaming with the hair on my head and the back of my neck standing straight up.

That is the only thing I am afraid of. I smoke more cigars because the smoke scares the spirits away, so they say. Still, I smoke. I smoke loads of cigars. I make my own cigars from dry grass. Smoking gives me a real buzz, or a huge headache.

Chapter 7

Battan

After Sealie dies, a man named Mr. Tom Hunter and his family come and live with us for a long time. I hate them all. I ask why this family, out of nowhere, has come to live with us. We have never heard of them before. We think that they are hiding something or from someone. Our first thoughts are that they are hiding from the government.

There is a man with Mr. Hunter named Lox. We always wonder who Lox is. We think he is Mr. Hunter's son because he's always with Philip, the other son. Lox does not look Spanish at all. He is Caucasian, and so is Philip, with their blond hair.

The villagers do not like Lox because he's too quiet. He does not mingle with them. Lox keeps to himself and always stays next to Philip. These two are always together. The villagers notice that, so they come to ask Dolores who these men are who are staying—living—with her.

The self-appointed mayor of the Rio Tinto, JoJo, claims to have a photo that resembles this man Lox, but no one believes it. Who would have a picture of a man who resembles Lox in Rio Tinto? Who would come to Rio Tinto and hide? We have never seen anyone here from the outside. So everyone just forgets about the claim.

I become very jealous because I keep seeing Dolores and Lox so close. They're always talking secretly together. I make it very clear to both of them that I do not like it. Whenever Dolores goes out of town to visit her parents, Lox takes her on the five-hour ride up river in the canoe. This burns me, keeps me wondering, *Is my mother in love with Lox?* I even tell Lox once, in front of Dolores, that I'm not going to tolerate anyone coming from the outside and giving me orders, and that I will try to eliminate his existence. They just think I'm crazy from picking too many coconuts or having too much moonshine. They do not pay too much attention to this dirty-faced eight-year-old kid.

Whenever Lox goes to pick coconuts with me, I get so irritated and try to stay away from him. I tell him not to come close to me, to leave me alone. I call him "long hair." I think he does not like that, but he laughs. He does not like getting dirty, so I try to get him dirty all the time by letting him pick coconuts instead of me. He gets irritated, and I laugh and make fun of him.

Lox is outwardly affable, in his mid-forties, and doesn't talk much. He has long shoulder-length black hair, is fair skinned and is very skinny. He and Phillip are always together. The only positive thing I can say about Lox is that he has a talent for playing the guitar. He is awesome at it! I find out at some point that he is hiding from the government. He was one of the generals in the rebel army that tried to overthrow the government, but it went bad.

He complains to Dolores about me, and I do not care. I have so much hatred toward Dolores because we did not go to Utila as she promised. We were going to leave this godforsaken coconut plantation, and instead she decides to stay and fight the townspeople for the land—For what? I'm tired, and I know what's coming. They're going to try to take advantage of us knowing that Sealie is no longer with us.

I'm tired of getting up in the morning and facing the same old brush. No matter where I look, all I see is jungle, and that's what I face every day, every morning—nothing but coconut trees, and lots of them, and lots of coconuts to pick. I never go to school—my excuse is that I have to pick coconuts. I hate school. If I go to school, there's no one to pick coconuts. And that works. The whole place is nothing but jungle. I'm sick and tired of being bitten by mosquitoes and fighting the elements.

One time Dolores and I go to Tela. She buys a ten-foot wagon to make it easier to transport the coconuts. It costs four hundred dollars. I think that's a lot of money, but she pays it, loads it on a boat, and brings it to Rio Tinto. It just sits there for I-don't-know-how long. We are afraid to use it, and we do not know how to use it. Not even Lox knows how to use it. I know what it's for, but I think that I'm dumb for not knowing how to use a wagon. It just sits there, collecting dust.

I'm not happy with these people in your home but there is nothing I can do about it. I hate them! They come out of nowhere giving me orders as if they own me. So, I go and play with the monkeys. They seem to have taken me in, and they feel comfortable with me. I touch them and groom them, like they do to each other. I keep the mosquitoes away from them. I find solace with them. I find comfort being with them. I stay with them for hours just to get some relief in my head.

The monkeys eat a wild fruit called *canepa*. It's a yellow fruit and it is good. I know where to find them. I climb the trees just like the monkeys, jump from tree to tree, make noises just like them, and jump up and down just like them.

One time, I'm jumping from tree to tree, and I'm going too fast. I miss the other tree, and I fall to the ground. I hurt myself very badly, and I lie there in extreme pain. All the monkeys come to comfort me. They make lots of noise. It sounds like they are laughing at me. They putting my head in their laps, and looking for bugs on me. I feel so comforted. I stay lying there for hours. I can't get up, and I do not feel anything. Finally, I fall asleep.

I feel as though these monkeys are my real family. I feel loved. I feel as if they care. I know that they are animals, but they have more feeling than my own family, my own parents. I never feel afraid of them even though there are some that are especially aggressive. The mean monkeys stay away from me because the rest keep them away. This is the real thing. They are so noisy; I can hear them for miles. Every time something happens to them, they make noise. Even the birds get scared, and they all fly away.

I go fishing one time with some of the villagers, deep-sea fishing, fishing for big game fish. There are lots of fishing hooks all over the canoe. I'm barefooted, and I stand up to get to the other side of the canoe and I step on a fishing hook. I scream. It's a hook for sharks, and the hook goes through the heel of my right foot to the bone. It's very deep. It starts to rain, and my blood washes all over the canoe. I feel like I'm going to pass out from the pain.

The men do not know how to take the hook out, so they take me to the village. Everyone rushes to see what's happening. They take me out of the canoe very carefully and lay me down on the sandy beach. I lie there in such agony, and they examine the damage. Every time someone touches it, I scream.

There are no doctors. All I hear is the villagers asking each other, "How do we take this out?" The hook is in deep. I think I'm going to lose my foot because no one knows what to do.

Here I lie, for hours it seems. Everyone is trying to figure out what to do, talking among themselves. I'm thinking, *Help me, help me! Get this thing out of me, don't just look at it!* I feel the blood draining from my face and body. I'm pale.

Out of nowhere, I feel a sharp pain in my head. Someone has hit me over the head to knock me out. I don't feel anything. When I wake up later, I'm home in bed with my foot all wrapped up in sheets. The sheet is wet with blood. I try to feel and to see if I still have a foot. I call for Dolores, and she comes and tells me that the men have taken out the hook by cutting through the skin and into the bone. I pass out again.

I don't know how long I've been out. I wake up, and Dolores tells me that I need to get up and go pick coconuts. I'm wondering, *How can I get up out of bed? I'm still bleeding!* I try anyway limping and fall to the ground. I cannot get my balance. I get dressed; grab my machete and the burlap sack, tie them across my shoulders, and off I go, limping using a stick for a cane.

I'm not moving too fast. My foot starts to bleed, and I just sit against a coconut tree and wait until it stops. It seems as though it will never stop. I crawl home and tell Dolores that I cannot do anything. I'm miserable, but she will not hear of it. Dolores burns a small sheet on an open fire. She takes the wrapping off of the wound, all this blood pours out. She takes the ashes from the sheet, fills the open wound with the ash, and then closes it and wraps it again. I'm screaming wildly. It feels like torture.

The next day, she opens the dressing again, and the bleeding has stopped. She washes the wound and wraps my foot back up. Lox comes in the door and tells me to stop being a little chicken and go pick coconuts. He's laughing. I want to kill him.

It takes a long time for my foot to heal, but I never stop going to pick coconuts, even though I'm limping. The coconuts need to be picked. My life depends on it. I don't know why—we're not selling that many coconuts anymore. They're no longer worth much.

On any given day, we pile the coconuts throughout various parts of the plantation. We make huge mounds of coconuts. We put five or ten, depending on the size of the coconuts, into burlap sacks. We carry them on our shoulders for two or three miles to the house. Lox gets tired of carrying only a few at a time, so he decides to use the wagon. It'll be the first time we try it.

We have a horse named Battan. He is a very strong horse, huge and muscular. He's a light orange color. He's an awesome horse. I love Battan. He's my horse. But, every time I mount Battan he throws me off his back. I go flying, so I'm also scared of Battan.

Lox asks me to go get Battan to hook the wagon to him. I reluctantly do what he tells me. I bring Battan to him. Battan, as soon he gets near Lox, starts to act up. He rears up on his hind legs and is being very difficult to control. I'm watching this and I tell Lox to stop and let the horse get used to him. Lox does not listen to me. The horse, after a while, settles down and is a bit easier to handle. Lox hooks the wagon Battan's back.

The horse stands there with the wagon attached to its back, not moving. He keeps turning to look to see what's attached to his back. It's about ten in the morning. We do not have clocks, but I figure that's the time. Lox grabs a heavy, thick stick and hits my horse on the butt. The horse jumps but doesn't move forward. Lox keeps hitting him. I try to tell Lox to stop hitting the horse, but it seems as though he's enjoying it.

Lox is now whipping the horse on his rib cage. The horse keeps jumping and is still not moving forward. He keeps looking to see what this huge thing is attached to his back. Lox is beating the horse harder and harder. Philip steps in and begins to slap and hit Battan with the flat blade of his machete. I'm screaming for them to stop. The horse is struggling, still not going anywhere. They finally stop . . . for now.

Battan is foaming at the mouth and I'm getting more and more worried. Battan is getting tired. Lox turns around, looks at me, and slaps the horse one more time on the buttocks. By this time, I'm calling Lox and Phillip and Dolores every foul name I know. Lox removes the wagon from the horse, grabs the horse's face, and starts squeezing the horse's eyes. I can't believe what I'm seeing, Lox reaches over the horse's neck and tries to get him in a headlock, tries to choke him. Dolores is watching this whole time, not saying anything. I'm cursing all of them, and finally Lox lets go.

Dolores sends me to pick coconuts. Lox and Philip stay there with Battan. I do not like that. I'm anxious about what they'll do next. I leave to go pick coconuts and I stop to look backward to see what they're doing. Lox ties two logs to the back of the horse, one on each side, to see how the horse reacts. The horse is not moving. He just stands there.

Later that afternoon, Lox fastens the wagon to the horse again, and again the horse does not move. I tell Lox that he needs to train the horse to get used to something on his back. I say, "Try and see if you can pull the wagon yourself." He doesn't like that.

The horse has the wagon attached to his back, Philip is pulling the horse, and Lox is hitting the horse with just about anything that he can get his hands on. The horse is not moving. Finally, the horse moves ahead a few steps.

Lox is having a field day whipping the horse to make him move. I'm screaming at Lox, cursing at him, but Lox keeps thrashing my poor Battan.

They finally get halfway to where we will load the wagon with coconuts. The horse stops. Philip pulls the horse from the front, and Lox continues to beat the horse. Battan goes down on his two front legs. Philip pulls hard to try to get the horse to stand up. Lox keeps whipping Battan's ribs, and it's killing me to watch the amount of abuse that these two guys are giving to my strong horse.

At last, Battan gives up and lies down with the wagon still attached to his back. I scream at Lox to stop and remove the wagon. Lox refuses. I keep cursing at him and at Philip. Lox finally gives up and removes the wagon. But Lox isn't done. He's mad. He goes and gets a torch, lights it, and sets the horse's hindquarters on fire! I grab my machete and I swing it at Lox. He doesn't see it coming. I wanted to hit him with the sharp side of the machete but I miss. Lox sets Battan's tail on fire. I run to Battan and try to put out the fire by throwing my body on top of him. Philip grabs me by my hair and pulls me away. I get away and try run to comfort my horse, and to put the flames out.

Philip grabs a handful of dry shrubs, and lays it by the horse's chest and sets it on fire. The horse does not move. They are beating the horse while he is on fire! The flames are growing and Battan's mouth is full of white foam.

I put the fire out, by stomping on it and hitting it with my hands. I lie there for hours trying to comfort him. I rest the horse's head on my lap. My face is black from soot, smoke and dirt, and I'm sobbing. I'm still cursing at Lox and Philip. They stand there watching me as I cry and comfort my poor Battan.

I stand up, grab my machete, and point it at Lox. I say to him, "I will grow up one day! When I do, I will hunt for you! And I will kill you! I will do to you what you've done to this horse! I want to see how you like it! So you better run!" Lox stands there with a smirk on his face. Philip is smirking too. They walk away laughing.

There is a hug mud pit where the pigs bathe. I run to mud pit and I grab some gobs of mud, I cover myself with it to keep the mosquitoes off. I go get a few coconut fronds and spread mud on them. I take them over to Battan and cover the burnt areas of his body. I'm fully covered with mud; only my nose and lips are exposed. I stay there comforting Battan. He's in a lot of pain. I can see it in his eyes and in his face. The horse is no longer the light orange color. He looks black from all the soot and burned skin. Oh, how I cry and cry!

I go home later that evening, but before I leave, I cover the burned areas with lots of coconut fronds. I make sure that the horse is clean by cleaning his mouth and the burned areas with water, very gently. Battan is breathing very hard, and I think he's going to die from the abuse; and for nothing—all because of two senseless, idiotic, cruel characters who think they know everything.

I yell at Dolores, but she does not say anything. It makes me even angrier that she does not say anything. I know she supports them.

I go back and stay by Battan late into the night. I'm tired of crying, and I'm feeling incredibly hateful. At the same time, I wish I could take the pain away from my poor Battan. I make a tent from coconut fronds to keep the horse cool at night and so the burn areas will stay covered. I leave him late into the middle of the night to go to bed.

The next day, early in the morning, I run out of the house looking for Battan, but he's not there. I search and search. I thinking the worst, I think the tigers have eaten him.

I finally find him. He is on his feet, eating grass. I'm so happy! I go near him and when he sees me, he rears up on his two hind legs. He seems to be scared of me at first but then he approaches me slowly, he is breathing hard, I know that Battan is going to be okay. I start to pet him and tend to his wounds. He lets me care for him as he continues eating. I take Battan away into the Jungle and hide him from Lox and Philip.

I despise them for what they have done. I have no respect for either one of them. I want to kill them, and I tell them so as often as I can.

CHAPTER 8

The Escape

I'm sitting in the kitchen around eleven o'clock in the morning. I'm facing toward the ocean. I hear harsh language coming from outside. I try to ignore it, but I fear the worst. Lox and Philip are outside, and Dolores is washing clothes outside, close to the house. She's visible from the closest neighbor's house. I keep ignoring all the foul language I hear toward Dolores. She keeps washing clothes, ignoring it as well. I look outside to see what's happening, and I see Geronimo at a neighbor's house, drunk, yelling toward our house, waving a gun, and swearing at Dolores. He's calling her all sorts of dirty names for letting Lox and Philip live with us. Geronimo is a Garifuna man, a bald man in his mid-fifties, somewhat muscular. He's one of the few Garifuna that has made it of the village and traveled to live in New York for a time and returned to live in Rio Tinto.

I try to ignore what is happening, thinking that it will pass. I do not want to deal with a man waving a gun. As I sit at the kitchen table, I see Geronimo leave on his horse, bareback, heading toward the beach. I think it's over.

At around two that afternoon, Lox, Philip, and I are getting ready to go and pick coconuts. Lox and Philip are getting their gear. I'm next to the wagon, getting my things together and sharpening my machete. I'm still afraid to go pick coconuts. I do not want to go. I hate Lox. Philip is standing next to me. I'm minding my own business.

Philip looks at me and says in Spanish, "You really want to make sure your machete cuts well."

I turn to look at him. I take the machete, I put it against my lips, I slide my tongue against the sharp edge, and I say to him, "This is for you!"

Suddenly, I hear voices coming from the neighbor's house. I turn around and I see Geronimo, waving his gun at us again. He is obviously drunk. Now he's calling Lox, challenging him to a gunfight. He's bragging about how good he is with a gun. He's calling Lox foul names, and he's saying he'll turn Lox in to the authorities for trying to over throw the Government. He says he knows Lox is a fugitive hiding from the government and he'll turn him in if he doesn't accept the gunfight challenge. Lox tries to look like he is minding his own business. I'm more concerned about going to pick coconuts than a drunken man waving a gun.

I hear is a loud bang. I turn around to see Geronimo aiming the gun at us. I hear another popping noise as something hits one of the wagon's wheels. I dive under the wagon. I see Lox pulling out his gun, returning fire. It seems like the bullets just keep coming. Lox runs out of ammunition. I stay under the wagon, covering my head. Philip runs to the house to get more bullets. He manages to sneak back and give them to Lox. While Lox is trying to reload, Geronimo just keeps firing at us. The next bullet hits another wheel. At this time, I decide to try to escape. I look around, deciding where to run. I see a wide tree nearby. I take off toward it and I hear a bullet hit it. I duck and cover my head. I look around trying to find where to go next. Lox and Geronimo just keep firing at each other.

I run toward a coconut tree, and I hide behind it. I hear bullets flying, my heart is pounding, I fear the worst. I'm worrying only about myself at this time. I look around again, wondering where to run next. There's a corral nearby, but it has barbed wire around it. I notice that there's a small gap at the bottom of the fence I could crawl under. I sprint toward it. I try to slide under the barbed wire, but my foot gets snagged. I'm panicking, my heart's pounding out of my chest. I can hear it! I'm dirty-faced and sweating. I think I'm going to die. I am able to get the barbed wire off of my foot, but I'm barefooted, so I'm bleeding. I run for cover toward the bushes and then I'm able to make it into the corral and under a pile of dry coconut branches. I burrow under them, and I stay there for a while listening. The ants are biting me, but I don't want to move. I'm afraid to move. I don't care. I'm hesitant to come out, but I decide I need a safer place and move to a nearby ditch where there are bushes all around for cover. I cover myself by scooping dirt on top of me.

I stay there for quite a while after the shooting stops. It seems like forever. I come out very slowly. I brush the dirt off, and look around. It's very quiet—too quiet, I think. I hear no voices. I'm expecting the worst, and I'm praying to God that nothing bad has happened to my family and hoping that Lox and Phillip are dead. I look around. There's no sign of anyone. I'm afraid that something bad has happened. I stop under a mango tree and I look toward the house. There's no sign of anyone. I run under the steps, and I don't hear any noises from anyone, not even the kids.

I think that they've all been killed. My heart is racing. I creep up the steps, very slowly and very quietly. I hear the rest of the kids in the front of the house and then I hear Dolores' and Lox's voices. Everyone seems to be alive! I thank God that nothing bad has happened to my family.

I'm bleeding. Dolores tries to clean my wound. I ask her what happened, and she tells me that Geronimo was shooting at them, but no one has been hit. I'm relieved, but the matter is not over yet. She tells me that Geronimo promised he'd come back later. She says Geronimo is after my family because he wants our land. Now that my father is dead, he wants to control the land and us. He has been somewhat educated in New York and feels he has the power to run us out and take our land.

All day I have been afraid for my life, for our lives. I don't know what Geronimo is going to do. I stay under the counter in the front store in front of the house, looking toward the center of the village, watching for Geronimo—I cannot stop watching. Finally, in the distance, I see a group of men coming with torches and machetes, marching toward our house.

I know this is going to be bad. I run and tell Dolores to come and see what is happening. She opens the front door and sees the men coming closer and closer. She closes the door and tells all of us to quickly close all the windows and doors. We all run to follow her orders. I run back to peer through the small hole to see what's happening. I see Geronimo approaching the house with about twenty to thirty men from the village, carrying torches, machetes, and clubs. They're chanting.

"We want Lox! We want Lox!" the crowd shouts.

Geronimo says, "Dolores, if you give us Lox, we will leave you alone. We have no problem with you. We loved Sealie! We want Lox."

Geronimo stops at the bottom of out stairs with a torch and his machete, waving them at us. I see some of the men come around to circle the house. I'm afraid they might set the hut on fire. I know most of them; I have played with their kids.

Geronimo yells, "Dolores! Dolores, I know you are there hiding Lox! We want to see Lox! Send him out, and everything is going to be okay!"

I'm watching all of this through the small hole. I'm scared, and my heart racing.

Geronimo says, "I will give you until nine o'clock tonight. I want Lox at that time. If not, we will come in and kill all of you, including the children, and we will burn the house down! You have until nine o'clock!"

The crowed chants, "We want Lox! We want Lox!" waving their machetes and torches. They have surrounded the house. I think we're all going to die. I beg Dolores to hand Lox over. I tell her we have nothing to lose. She gets mad at me for suggesting this, but I don't care. He's of no use to me. After what he and Philip did to my horse, I want to get rid of him.

As the crowd begins leave, Dolores and Lox try to come up with a plan.

I tell Dolores, "What plan? Hand him over, or let's run to the woods."

I just want to get out of the house before they come back, but Geronimo is staying near the house. He is outside one of the neighbor's houses watching us to make sure no one leaves.

I want to go now! I don't want to wait with them. It's almost nightfall. Six o'clock comes, seven o'clock comes, eight o'clock comes; we're still in the house. By this time, there's a full moon, and it's very bright. Lox and Dolores say to get ready, that before nine o'clock, we're going to leave for the woods. There isn't much to pack, and there isn't enough time to pack much.

While Dolores and Lox are making final plans to get out of Rio Tinto, Philip is just stands around waiting to see what we do. I keep watch under the counter and try to keep track of everyone. I think to myself, *I know all these people, I play with their kids, and I have spent lots of time in their homes. They worked for us. Most of them worked for Ernest or Sealie in the past. But now they want to run us out of our home or kill us. Now I can't trust any of them. As far as I'm concerned, they are my enemies, every one of them.*

Dolores gathers all of us while Lox sharpens his machete and checks his gun, and collects his bullets. Philip looks on. I have my machete ready, and as scared as I am, I will have no problem killing anyone who crosses my path.

Dolores says, "We are leaving here before nine o'clock."

Lox says, "It's a full moon, they might see us leaving the house. Philip, go out and hide behind the shed. See that no one approaches the house. If they come close to the house, throw a rock at the door. It's a bright moon and they might see us, but we will try to go. We will head toward the plantation, and then toward the beach."

Philip sneaks outside using the kitchen door and hides behind the shed with his machete in hand, looking toward the center of the village.

Lox then says, "We will walk toward the beach. When Philip joins us, he will go ahead of us, checking all the canoes along the beach. We are all going to walk in a line. Sealie you go first, Janelle second, George you're third, Kelly you go last. Dolores, you carry Jacinta. I will walk in the back." Carmela and Saina are not with us at the time. My mother has sent them to live with her parents.

"If anything happens—they may come after us—we may not have a chance," Lox continues. "They could be hiding inside the canoes on the beach. If you see them coming after us, all you kids jump in the water and try to hold your breath. I don't think they will follow you into the water. Try to swim if you can. If not, hold your breath. Hope for the best. We will meet at the river. So do we all have it down? Okay! Lots of luck!"

I say to him, "You're wishing us luck? Why are you wishing us luck? Are you going to leave us in the middle of the ocean? Is that your plan?" I don't know why I say this.

We all sneak down the front stairs. The moon is very bright. We are straining to see ahead of us and we looking behind us to see if anyone is following. Lox walks with caution and his gun drawn. I have my machete. Dolores has Jacinta on her hip. Jacinta is only a year old. She starts to cry and to cough. Dolores tries to stop her by putting a cloth in her mouth.

We're all terrified, and we wonder if we can make it. We think that maybe they are waiting by the river to finish us off. We walk past their houses, along the beach. Philip walks ahead of us, checking in the canoes that are lined up along the riverbank. We notice the big outboard motor that they have on their boats compared to what we have. We won't have a chance if they chase us in our boat with such a small motor.

After walking what seemed like hours, Lox and Philip push our small canoe onto the water. There's a family there that we know and Dolores tells them should anyone ask for us, to tell them they have not seen us.

It's now about eleven o'clock at night. We get in the canoe, and push off. The moon is still very bright. We start rowing so that no one hears the motor of the boat. I duck down on the floor of the canoe to hide.

After a few miles, we start the canoe's engine and are going very slow. Suddenly we hear a noise like thunder. We're not sure what it is, so Lox shuts off the engine, and we listen. We realize that it's not thunder; it's the noise of fast outboard motors. They are coming after us! We panic. We do not know where to hide or where to go. We decide to head for the cover of the shrubs along the edge of the river. The moon is still bright.

We paddle the canoe toward the riverbank and hide behind the green brush. We all crouch down and are trying to be quiet. Jackie sneezes. Dolores tries to stop her. I'm on the floor of the canoe, trying to be quiet and wondering what is going to happen.

We hear their outboard engines coming closer. We hold our breaths, trying to be quiet. They come close. We see them go by, and then they stop and shine a flashlight over bushes on the riverbank. We see the beam coming toward us, so we get down and hope they do not see us.

They start their engines again, and then they pass by us. A short time later, they come back again. We hear crocodiles in the water and see some of them coming toward the canoe. Geronimo's men are still looking for us. Lox goes to shore and grabs a stick and tries to scare the crocodiles away. We wait some more and then we hear the engines again. They get close, and a bright light shines along the shore again.

We wait for what felt like hours and decide that all is clear and quiet enough to move. We come out from behind the thick shrubs, and start to paddle out. After a while, we start the engine again. By this time, we're exhausted.

It's now about one in the morning, and it's very dark. We can hardly see where we are going on the river. We go on instinct. We get to the end of the river at about three in the morning. Now we have to climb a steep river bank. We are tired, and hungry, trying to climb this steep, slippery bank.

We make it up and now we do not know where to stay. Dolores goes and knocks on the door of a friend's hut, we have stayed here before. They open the door at three in the morning. They let us come in, and sleep on the dirt floor. We're cold, but we don't care; we're tired and hungry. But there's no time to think of food. Just having a place to stay at three in the morning is a relief.

This has been the longest night of my life. I think that Geronimo is going to show up in the morning when we go to catch the train. I feel bugs crawling on my head. They feel so big, and I'm trying to fight them off. I fall asleep.

The next morning, it's pouring rain. It feels like the skies opened up. We are dirty. We walk toward the train station through the mud. We're getting soaked, but I don't care. I just want to get on that train. I don't care where it takes us. Once we're on board and the train is in motion, we should be safe.

Those who have shoes put them on, but some of us are barefoot, walking in the red mud. It's very slippery. It's like clay. We walk to the station, which is not far but difficult to get to in the rain. We wait for the train for an hour. Many people are waiting with their livestock—pigs, chickens, cows, and goats.

Some of the travelers have machetes hanging from their shoulders and have various cuts on their faces, arms, and legs. I scan the crowd thoroughly to see if I see Geronimo. I'm cold and still not at ease. I feel like until I'm on that train, I'm not safe.

Finally, the train approaches the station. It couldn't have come at a better time! It's a good feeling to see this train, and I'm starting to feel hopeful we will be safe. The train pulls into the station and we board. It's packed with people. There are hardly any seats left. There is a man with one arm, with a machete hanging from one shoulder and two white-handled guns hanging from his hips. I feel like asking him to give me one of his guns. He gets up and offers his seat to Dolores. He moves to the next car.

We are more comfortable now, but we keep vigilant, looking for Geronimo in case he decides to board the train at one of the stops. We're comfortable for the twenty-five-mile train ride. We're going to La Union, to Dolores's parents' house. They live way up in the mountains. No one can find us there, no one. The jungle there is dense and wild. I'm so tired. I look around at the people, and then I put my head on Dolores's shoulder and pass into a deep sleep.

The train pulls into the station in La Union. It feels like I've been asleep for a long time, and now we have to walk a long way, about six miles, to my grandparent's house. I'm tired and hungry. I do not want to do anything. Everyone is exhausted. You can tell by looking at us that we're beat.

When the train comes to a full stop, some of the people get off with their chickens, goats, and pigs. It's a very busy station, and we have to wait until most of the people disembark so we can get off too. We get off the train, and we're all disoriented from the long trip. I don't want to go any further. I want this ordeal to be over, but I know that it has probably just begun.

We stop at a nearby café and order a bottle of Coke. We sit down, and I'm noticing the local people who are walking up and down with their livestock, going about their own business. The manager of the café seems to be a busy guy. He has two guns on his waist. He's a happy-go-lucky guy, talking loud, giving lots of orders to everyone. He comes to me and asks me my name, and then he walks away because someone has called him. I don't know where he gets his energy and wish I had some of it now.

There are fruit trees all over his property and he comes back to tell me to go and pick whatever fruit I want off his trees. I get up and go pick some fruit, and I eat a few pieces. I'm so hungry. I'm also sweaty and not looking forward to walking again.

I keep thinking that when we get to my grandparents' house, I can relax. It's a hot afternoon. We have to walk along the railroad tracks for a mile or so. Along the way we have to cross a bridge, but the railroad ties are very far apart. I fear I might fall through one of the spaces to my death below.

We're all sweating, and walking along the railroad is not fun. It's hot and I can feel the heat rising off the railroad tracks. From time to time, a railroad security car will pass by, and we have to stop and watch it pass.

We have to walk through cattle corrals and over a high hill to get to Dolores's parents' house. When we come to the area where we have to cross the corral, we each have to go under a barbed-wire fence. Philip holds up the fence so each of us can pass through. There is a large herd of cattle in the corral, and I see a few bulls looking at us menacingly. I try to ignore them. We walk another half mile across the corral and out the other side and start to climb the steep hill.

We get to a narrow trail up and along the side of a mountain. It is hot, I'm tired, and we keep walking slow and steady, the trail overlooks the panoramic scenery of the green valley below and the railroad tracks in the distance. We reach the top and can finally see the valley below where Dolores's parents live. We can see the plume of smoke coming from their chimney. It is a great sight to see.

I'm thinking now I can relax and sit down for once in a long while. We descend the steep hill, and stop at a beautiful waterfall. I run toward it and jump with my clothes on into the water and try to cool off. It's fantastic! The water is sweet and refreshing. I don't want to get out. I'm having too much fun playing in the waterfall. Dolores calls me to come out of the water.

We get to Dolores's parents' house, and there her father greets us—Lox, Philip, all of us. He shows us the cattle ranch. He has over five hundred head of dairy cattle he uses to make cheese. With all the men working for him, I figure he has lots of money.

I find a corner somewhere in the house on the clay floor. I sit down and think, *No one can find us here. No one knows about this place, it's out of the reach of anyone!* I take a deep breath. I'm glad to be in a place where I can rest without having one eye open. I close my eyes and fall asleep.

After a few days at Dolores's parents' house, Dolores and I go to Tela, Atlántida. It is the nearest city and oversees the district of Rio Tinto. We walk into the police station and ask for *el teniente* (Lieutenant) Bonilla. He was one of Sealie's friends. Every time Bonilla went to Rio Tinto, we would provide his men with a place to stay. They would stay in tents outside on our property. Whenever Sealie went to Tela, they would get together for a beer or two.

We enter the police station ask for *el teniente* Bonilla. I'm sitting in the lobby. It's early afternoon. Dolores is at the counter asking for Bonilla when Geronimo walks in. We're surprised. I'm so shocked to see him walk in I suck in my breath and hold it. I cannot believe it! To see Geronimo, of all the people, of all times, we pick that day to go to the police station. I'm sucking a lollipop, my mouth opens and it drops to the floor.

He walks in, and he looks happy, as if nothing has happened. He says, "Hello, Dolores! How are you this wonderful day! It's a wonderful day, yes indeed. What are the both of you doing in the police station? I'm so happy to see the both of you."

Dolores says, "I'm here to file a police complaint against you. Good thing you're here so we can talk to *el teniente* Bonilla."

Geronimo says, "Bonilla, he is my best friend! I know him."

I hear this and I start to shake. I even wet myself. I think that he is going to try to hurt us again. I do not know what to do or where to go.

Geronimo says, "I want to buy you both some refreshments. I'm so excited to see you, Dolores! This is a real treat for me and a surprise to see you both here!"

Dolores tells him, "You need to leave us alone."

"Dolores! I just want to tell you how sorry I am to hear about Sealie. If there's anything that I can do, let me know!"

The police station clerk is listening. He says, "I'm sorry to tell you, but *el teniente* is not here but, you can file a complaint if you step inside."

Geronimo walks out of the police station with a smirk on his face. I watch him as he's leaving. He stops, turns around, looks at me, and we make eye contact. Then he smiles and waves at me. I can't believe what I'm seeing.

I walk with Dolores into the clerk's office. Dolores files the complaint. The clerk tells her he cannot do anything, and that it is out of the jurisdiction of *el teniente*.

She asks for protection and a military escort upon return to Rio Tinto. They refuse. They tell her that they do not have enough personnel for a military escort.

She says to them, "What about all the times *el teniente* Bonilla and his men went to Rio Tinto? The times we fed them and gave them a place to stay?"

The clerk says, "I'm sorry, but I can't give you an escort in order for you to return to your property. I feel for you. If you want to go to Tegucigalpa to see the commandant of the army, you certainly can do so"

We leave the station disappointed, not knowing what to do now. We take the evening express train to San Pedro Sula. It's late. I'm wet, hungry, and exhausted. I think we're finished—we have no case against this man. I see all these women, men, and children selling food in the streets at every stop. Dolores buys food along the way at one of the stations.

When we arrive in San Pedro Sula, we take a taxi to Dolores's brother's house. Anthony takes us in and we tell him what they told us in Tela. I hear Dolores tell him we're going to Tegucigalpa in the morning.

We are up early to catch the bus to the capital. On the bus, we are packed in like sardines. The bus is so full people are sticking their heads out of the windows to catch a breath of fresh air. They keep packing in the people. I wonder, *How many more sardines are they going to fit in this can?*

It takes us five hours to get to the capital. We take a taxi to the army headquarters where Dolores asks for the army commandant. The clerk tells us to take a seat and asks why we are there.

Dolores says, "I want to file a complaint against a man by the name of Geronimo in the district of Rio Tinto, Tela Atlántida."

The clerk repeats, "Take a seat."

We sit for about twenty minutes. I feel apprehensive that they will deny us security.

The commandant comes out and asks us to enter his office. We sit in his leather chairs. It's a very plush office. I've never seen anything like it. It's beautiful!

The commandant asks, "How can I help?"

Dolores tells him, "I want to file a complaint against a man by the name of Geronimo, in the district of Rio Tinto, Tela."

The commandant says, "What did this Geronimo do for you to come this far up in the chain of command?"

Dolores tells him, "He has run us off our property in the district of Rio Tinto. I want to see if you can give me a military escort to the village."

The commandant asks, "Where is this Rio Tinto that you're referring to?" He calls for his assistant and asks for him to bring a map.

The assistant hands the map to the commandant. He opens it, looks at it, and says, "I don't see the village that you're talking about here on this map!"

"It's by Tela."

"I've never heard of this village before." He keeps looking at the map. "I don't see it. If it is by the city of Tela, I'm sure it's there, but I have never heard of it. It's out of our jurisdiction, if it's here. It has to be under the jurisdiction of Tela." He looks at Dolores. "I'm sorry, but I can't help you with any escort!"

This is our last effort, and Dolores and I leave very disappointed.

Dolores says to me, "I guess we are going back. This time when they come after us, I'm killing them. They are dead." She looks serious.

Upon our return to San Pedro Sula, we return to Uncle Anthony's and she tells him what the commandant said.

Anthony says, "I'll go with you to Rio Tinto. I will kill anyone who tries anything!"

Anthony is in his late fifties, with black hair—or at least he says he's got black hair. He dyes it. He walks with a limp. He likes guns, and he has a pair of beautiful ivory-handled guns at his house. He enjoys Hitler's philosophy.

Dolores agrees to his help.

Anthony says, "These people are not going to mess with you. I will kill them all as soon as they look at me wrong, I will kill them! They are not going to mess with me. I have my guns. They are my treasure! I don't ask questions. I will kill and then ask questions!" He laughs.

The next day, my mother and I walk over to the station to catch another train. It's not an express train, so the train stops at every stop to load people with their goods to take to other cities to be sold.

After an exhausting train ride, we arrive at Treinta y Dos. Here, we now have to see if anyone is going to Rio Tinto. Dolores finds some people who are friendly and she asks them if they are going to Rio Tinto. They nod their heads yes, so we board their small canoe and they start paddling another four or five hours to get home.

As we ride along the river, we see various animals like crocodiles feeding or just relaxing in the sun, and monkeys eating in trees. I try to make sounds like them to see if they notice us. The water on the river is dirty, muddy red.

There's a slow current so it helps us along the way. The man in the canoe is paddling, looking around very intensely. We hear the birds, something I never noticed in all the times we have been on this river. The scenery seems completely different from when we left a month earlier.

I'm wondering when we get home what we are going to find. *Is the house going to be burned? Where is my horse? That is going to be one of the first things I do when I get home—look for Battan.*

As the canoe approaches the riverbank, and I look around it seems very quiet, no one's around. I'm nervous. I'm looking hard at the thick brush nearby.

Anthony has his two guns on his waist. He looks like he's ready for action.

We get out of the canoe, we gather all of our belongings, and we start to walk the five miles home. We get home, and it looks so different now. I do not know what it is, but it's not the same as it was when we left. I feel like we have been robbed and violated.

At home, I find my machete, but I'm afraid to go to the plantation. I do not know what I'm going to find there, so I'm careful about where I go. I try to stay along the road, near the beach, in the open. I look for Battan.

I'm smoking a big cigar, and I feel the mosquitoes biting me. It's a hot afternoon. I keep searching, calling for Battan, but I cannot find him. I do not know where else to look for him.

I have my dog, Trivillin. I have forgotten about my dog! He is white with a dark spot over one eye. He's an extraordinarily faithful dog. He goes everywhere I go. I am not good to him though. He still stays next to me. I tell him to go look for Battan, and he does.

Later that evening, as I'm chopping wood, I see Battan running with another horse, they are playing. I'm so happy when I see him. He seems to be having fun, and he does not look like he's in any type of pain any longer. I go near him and round him in. I pull him next to a tree and I mount him bareback.

I ride him along the beach. He is galloping with no problem. We go faster and faster, and then he notices another horse on the loose. He runs toward it, rears up, and throws me off his back. I go flying and land in some wild berry bushes. I walk back home, limping.

It has been a week since our return and since Antonio has been with us. Things aren't going well. The natives are harassing us by coming at night and throwing firebombs at the house. He walks around the village with his two ivory-handled pistols. The villagers don't seem to like that. They have been coming to Dolores asking her why he's been seen around the village with his guns. Dolores tells them that he is her brother, and he likes walking around with his guns. Anthony doesn't talk much, and the villagers find that to be a form of disrespect toward them.

Geronimo seems to be quiet lately, but he has been sending his friends to do all the dirty work for him. One of Geronimo's brothers has been making his intentions well known by coming to the house and talking to Dolores telling her that he wants to marry her. He says he will take good care of her since she is now alone. He tells her to sell her house to him and that he will give her a great price. If she isn't going to sell, he will see to it that she is thrown out, one way or another. Anthony just listens to all of this, doing nothing but sharpening his machete.

Dolores gathers a few of the villagers and pays them to move all the lumber that Sealie had in storage to the back of the San Jose property.

After all the lumber is delivered, with the help of the people in the village, she starts to build a house. It's a big house with three bedrooms, a huge living room, and a kitchen and dining room. It looks like it is going to be a nice house. In only a few weeks, the house is taking shape.

One night there is pounding on our front door. It's one of the guys who is building the house. He tells Dolores that the new house is in flames. Even though it's the middle of the night, we run toward the burning house. It is dark, and there are a lot of thick shrubs along the way. We keep getting tangled in some of them. We can hardly see in the dark.

We get to the house, but we cannot do anything; it's gone. The flames are so big, and all we hear is the crackling of the fire that is burning the wood. All the extra lumber is in flames also. It lights up the midnight sky for miles. It's very intense. We stand there, watching the flames. We cannot do anything. This is the work of Geronimo. Anthony just stands there with his two guns on his waist.

I'm on the plantation with my dog, trying to catch iguanas to eat. I try catching a big one, but the dog cannot catch it. I set traps for the night around some of the coconut trees, these are the ones that some of the thieves go to.

Dolores has told me that Anthony is leaving in a few days and that I'll be going with him. I don't want to go. I like it here. I feel comfortable with my friends. I will miss the snakes I play with, the monkeys that have taken me in as a part of them. It has been great. I'm glad that they are still around, and they still remember me even though I have been gone for a few months. I will also miss Battan. I don't know what's going to happen to him when I'm gone.

I don't want to go. I want to stay here and work the land and live among my friends, the animals. At this point I don't know what to do; one part of me wants to leave this godforsaken place, the other part of me wants to stay. I want to take the care of the animals, my horse. I'm afraid of what is going to happen to them if I leave. Even though I hate it here, I may want to stay just to take care the horse. If I leave I know I will miss all of it. This is what is familiar and the city is not. Even though these people don't want us there, I'm sure I can grow up fast and fight them. I want to take over what we had. I miss Sealie. I feel like it's up to me to stand up to these people, let them know who is the man.

Dolores does not want me around. After all, I have been a bad son to her. I've been a thorn in her side. What good am I? I guess I'm no good for anything. The only thing I can do is pick coconuts. There's no place else I know of that has a coconut plantation or monkeys I can play with.

Even though Sealie was mean to me, I miss him very, very much. I cry because I no longer have my father. If he were alive, things would be great. The natives would leave us alone. They seemed to respect him to a certain extent.

God, what am I going to do with my life? Where am I going to end up? I'm good for nothing. Everything that has happened here is my fault.

My days here are coming to an end. I'm going to go and live with my grandparents. I hate living with them. I hear lots of stories about living with them, especially with Anthony around. He is a bully. He beats up kids with crowbars.

I wish I could bring my dog and Battan. I don't want to leave Battan alone. I have expressed this to Dolores, but she has her mind set. Why is she sending me away? I feel like I should stay for a while longer. There are issues that I have to settle with some of these people.

Someday I will grow up, and the first thing I will do, the first desire I will fulfill, is to look for Lox and get my revenge. I will remind him about what he did to Battan. Philip will be next! All of the mistakes I've made, now they are coming at me. The first mistake I think I made was being born, living in a rotten place like this, with no way out is another.

It's getting late, and I think I'd better go home—not that I have to go, because I have nothing to go to really. I don't want to listen to Dolores or Anthony. Maybe I should just run away. No one will notice. I'm leaving tomorrow, and I have nothing to take with me but my machete. Who knows what waits for me?

I'm leaving one bad home to go to another bad home. Since Sealie died, it seems as though we all need to go our separate ways. I'm sad looking at the ocean, looking at the plantation, maybe for the last time. I do not know what is going to happen to Battan. I love Battan. He has been a good horse, a strong horse. *God, keep him safe please. Don't let anything happen to him. Oh God! Please, help him. Thank you for bringing him back from the ordeal with Lox.*

The time for me to leave is getting closer. My dog! Who is going to care for him? He has been a very faithful dog. I should have paid more attention to him. I don't want to go. My life is coming to an end. What is going to happen to Rio Tinto, to the house? I have hated it here. But, we can hear the waves break from the hut, on a quit night or a quiet day, when the ocean is calm, you can hear the waves break very softly. I will miss that.

What happens from this moment on is not in my hands. My destiny is in who-knows-whose hands. I doubt the existence of God. If there is a God, why would he let this happened?

Well, this is the day, the day I have to say good-bye, the day to say good-bye to Battan, to Trivillin, to my brothers the monkeys—to the only family I have ever known.

Dolores says I have to go so I have to go. I may never come back and see Battan playing with the other horses. I don't hear the monkeys making any noise. I guess they are sad. We have to walk five miles to the river for the final time now. My dog is walking very slowly behind me. I don't want to look back. I don't want to look at him. I'm looking at all of this for the last time, never to set foot here again and never to find out what happens to Rio Tinto.

Anthony, the guy who move in and was going to stop Geronimo from taking advantage of us, didn't even last a week. He got scared. He's a city boy, and he does not like heavy work. He is all talk, no action. He could not do a thing!

We are walking very slowly. I don't want to go and leave all of this. I notice no one is out watching us leave. They must be hiding. It is very quiet. As we pass Ernest's house, it sits there very still, very quiet. What a place to have once seen! It's a place that once made so much money. It now sits in silence. Only memories lie inside his house now. No one looks after it, another disappointment in life. They had money, lots of money, and did not know what to do with it. They should have left some for the grandkids, but no!

I walk through the coconut plantation for the last time. The voices of the people who once worked here echo in my head. All this land that at one time produced millions of coconuts. It sits still in time, remembering all the sweat sacrifices each human who worked here made. These trees have produced wealth for those who wanted it. They were not able to take care of it, to nurture it. It is all lost now.

It has been a long walk to the river where we are about to part ways—me and Rio Tinto. Not knowing where my mother is, or if she even cares. It's sad and disappointing knowing that everything has been in vain. All that work, all the sacrifice each of us made is totally wasted, gone, finished. All the people who once prospered here, from the coconuts, all gone, nothing to show for it; only disappointing memories now. As I think about what waits for me, I'm very scared and my heart is broken.

As I get in the small canoe and look back, my dog is at the water's edge, crying. He jumps in the water, wanting to catch the canoe, but I would rather not feel anything or look. It is too hard for me to look at him, I would rather do what my parents have done with me—not look, not listen. The dog finally gives up and stands on the shore watching and howling. I pretend I don't hear it. It is almost impossible to endure. I tell myself, *Why should I let the dog get under my skin? I will only cry. I don't want to cry. I have to be strong—the way my parents made me—to feel nothing about anyone, not even the dog that is howling for me.*

Goodbye, Trivillin. I hope someone can take care of you. But I will never see you or hear you howling again. The dog runs along the shore, barking and, at times jumping into the water. When he sees that he can't catch up with the canoe, he runs back to the beach. He follows as far as he can.

From a distance I still hear him barking, but I pretend I do not hear him. I put my face on the grass pillow, and I start sobbing. The tears come from deep down. They keep flowing. I can't stop sobbing. I try to catch my breath.

I look at the river one more time, I listen to the man paddling, I see the people on land, and the houses that are being built at the far side of Ernest's property. I remember that this river is responsible for our escape from Geronimo and I hope I never have to go through that again.

What is the fate of Rio Tinto? Who knows? What is going to happen to Dolores? Is she going to survive against these people? I can't understand why she's staying behind with only the younger kids. Why is she sending me away? Have I been bad? I don't understand. I have no answers. It feels like everything that has happened has been my fault. This must be why she is sending me away.

I focus on the trees along the riverbank trying to see the monkeys I hear making noise along the way. The monkeys were once my real family, my brothers and sisters. I had fun playing with them. They made me laugh when I needed to laugh; they helped me forget about my sorrows and my problems. As I look at them, I feel like they are telling me good-bye, seeing me one last time. We will never see each other again. I see them jumping from tree to tree, following the canoe; all the birds in the trees make noise as if they are frightened. Tears roll down my cheeks as I remember all the fun times I had with the animals, as I think of how much I will miss them and much I want to stay. Anthony looks at me with a smile. I'm sobbing uncontrollably, *God! God! Take care them for me! Please! God!*

As we continue moving down the river, I look back and watch the current moving us along the muddy river. All of this should have been mine. I should have been living in a big house, living a good life, but thanks to my parents, it is not meant to be. The canoe keeps moving on to the mouth of the river as I sit there holding on to my grass pillow, tears rolling down my dirty face. I am miserable.

Finally, I see the end of our river journey ahead. It has been a long trip, and the pilot of our canoe makes his final approach to the riverbank. He centers the canoe. There are a few men on the shore with some chickens and a couple of goats, trying to load them onto their canoe. They say hello. I notice their machetes and the guns hanging from their shoulder holsters and waists. A few of them have fresh wounds on their bodies. The man in our canoe tells them that the current is very strong in some parts of the river. They acknowledge him.

We get out, walk up the bank and make our way to the train station, and here we sit until finally the train pulls up. It looks like a long train. We board along with many other people. Anthony still has his two guns on his waist. I sit down in a dazed. The train pulls out of the station, blows its whistle. I hear the wheels moving and the whistle blowing. I just sit there, quietly holding my grass pillow.

CHAPTER 9

The Orphanage

I have been living here with my grandmother in San Pedro Sula for two months, and I have hated every moment of it. There are too many kids here. All of my aunts' kids are living here, and my sisters Carmela and Saina live here too. I don't like my cousins. All they want to do is fight. They like to start fights. I just got here, and they have been living here for a long time, so they think that they can do whatever they want. My grandmother doesn't say anything, because she likes them better than she likes me.

There are seven kids here, so the house is full. Anthony tries beating us with a metal bar. We have to be in bed by eight o'clock, and if we're not, he chases us around the house with his metal bar. I miss Rio Tinto.

I have not heard anything from Dolores. Every day I get up not knowing the future holds for me. How long am I going to stay here in this hellhole?

I want to run away, just to get out of here. Out from under Anthony's thumb. He seems to be guarding the children. My grandmother comes and goes. She goes to her farm in La Union where my grandfather is most of the time. Anthony is always bullying us and harassing us. He walks around the house with his metal crowbar.

One day I'm in the street playing with the other kids, making the best of thing that I can—I tend to forget about Dolores in Rio Tinto and about life's worries when I play with the other kids, but I'd rather be playing with the wild monkeys in the jungle—when Anthony calls me into the house. He sits me down at the kitchen table and looks at me with his menacing eyes. I'm trembling just looking at him. I think that he is going to spank me. He starts to talk to me.

He says, "I need to tell you something. I have been told to tell you that you'll be leaving here. I'm taking you to a house, a big house, at the other end of the city where you'll be with other kids that are in your condition."

I ask, "What condition is that?"

He says, "Kids that are in need."

"What does that mean?" I say.

He continues, "I have been told that you'll be taken away. Maybe someone will adopt you."

I'm astounded, "So someone will be my mother and father again?"

Anthony simply says, "Yes."

I put my forehead down on the table; I'm looking down at the floor. I'm thinking that it never ends for me. I cannot stop sobbing, crying, wishing I had someone to love me. I know that there is no one to help me. Who would take a kid like me? According to Dolores, I have been bad. Is this my payment?

Anthony starts to get my few things together. I don't have much. There are only a few old-looking shirts and one pair of pants. I sit there sobbing. The older kids come in the house and into the kitchen. They see me sobbing and crying with my head down on the kitchen table. They ask Uncle Anthony what my problem is. Anthony tells them that I'll be leaving tonight, to the "big house."

They all know what he means by the "big house." I'm the only one who doesn't. I really don't know until one of the other kid's whispers in my ear that it's an orphanage. I don't know what to think. I had thought it was a vacation house, even though I knew it was going to be bad. It's not good to end up in an orphanage!

Anthony calls a taxi. When the taxi pulls in front of the house, Anthony calls me to come out. I walk toward the front of the house. All the kids are looking at me. I'm looking down. I do not want to look at them. I'm still sobbing. I cannot stop crying. I feel as if I'm being given away. No one wants me anymore, so they're putting me away to see if someone else will take me.

My sister Carmela is there, watching me walk with my head down. She does not say anything, not even good-bye. I'm expecting her to perhaps do something, but I guess I'm expecting too much from her. I'm dragging my feet. I do not want to go away. I don't know where this "big house" is, or what I'm going to do there, or what they do to you there. I cannot understand why I'm being taken, or being given away. What bad did I do to deserve this? Has Dolores said something to Anthony in order for him to do this?

I'm so torn apart inside. I don't know what the hell to do. I feel helpless. I want someone to do something to stop this, but I know that there is no one. I'm on my own. I'm going to the "big house" to see what will happen.

It's dark outside when I get in the taxi. I cover my face because I don't want the rest of the kids to see me. I'm inside the taxi, looking at the lights, blurry through my tears, as we drive. I'm wondering when we are going to get there. I'm cold and tired, and I want to sleep. I want to lie down in a bed. I don't know what to expect.

Anthony is sitting next to me, smiling. I hate that—seeing him with that smirk on his face. I want to slap it off of him. I feel like saying to him, "I'm being taken away to be given away. Can you do that? Just give someone away?"

It seems as though it's a long taxi ride. We get out of the taxi, and Anthony knocks on the door of the "big house." I'm looking at him, feeling scared, trembling. I don't want to go in. The door opens and a woman greets Anthony. She introduces herself as the principal of the place. Her name is Maria, she says. She welcomes us in, and she looks at me. I look around inside and do not see anyone else.

She says, "This must be the boy that you want to leave here with us."

Anthony says, "Yes, is name is Sealie! He is a good boy, but he needs to stay here with you for a while."

She says, "Well, welcome to our place. I hope you like it, playing with the rest of the boys!"

I'm tired, it's late at night, and I want to lie down and sleep. I'm also hungry, but I know that there's no food.

I keep looking around the room, taking everything in. I'm trembling; I cannot stop trembling. I'm biting my fingernails. Tears are still rolling down my face. I watch them talking like I'm in a dream. She's talking to Anthony, and I'm not listening. Not knowing what to expect, not knowing my fate I think that's the hardest.

Then, the meaning of "big house" really hits me. The other kids told me at my grandmother's house what it was, but for some reason it didn't sink in. This it's not good! Every day I'm breathing from this day forward is not going to be a good. I'm filled with dread. I want to die, get it over with. I know that no one will want to adopt me. The only people who could want me are the farmers to work on their banana plantations. I'm trained for the coconut plantation, and there's no way I'm going to go work on a banana plantation. No way. I'd rather stay here until I grow old.

I am holding my brown bag with a shirt and a pair of pants—the extent of my belongings. I am sitting, looking down, not listening, and thinking about where I went wrong. What did I do to end up here in this place where they bring kids when they don't want them or can't afford them?

A short time later, Anthony finishes filling out the paperwork. He looks at Maria, smiles and he leaves, never even looking at me. I watch him close the door. I feel as if I'm not worth anything, and I ask myself why I am alive. Is my destiny really behind those double doors into the orphanage?

Maria comes over, extends her hand to my chin, and lifts my head. I look at her with eyes full of tears, trembling, sobbing. It seems as though all I have done is sob. She looks at me, and then wipes away my tears.

She says, "It's going to be okay! I will see that nothing happens to you while you're here. Your name sounds very familiar to me. I know of a family that goes by the name of Lowell! It will be okay here, so no more crying."

I try to control myself, but I just can't stop sobbing. I know that I'm all alone now, despite what she's telling me. I know better. I know that being in a place like this is permanent. There's no way out unless someone comes looking for someone to be their slave. That is why people come to these places—to look for kids to be their slaves. I will be someone else's slave just to get out of here, any time!

I spend my days in the orphanage scrubbing walls, floors, benches, all over. I wear my old pair of pants and my old shirt. I think they are the same ones I wore when I came from Rio Tinto. This is not a nice place to be. There are about hundred kids in various rooms and halls, which are cold with wet floors. Each child sleeps on a tiny cot.

Once you get to a certain age in an orphanage, you're turned out to the streets. That's another thing to worry about—staying here until I turn fifteen. Then I'll end up on the streets, selling oranges or mangos, maybe selling monkeys. No, not them, they're my family.

I bite my fingernails to the quick. I try to be good, and from time to time the other kids play with me. I'm trying to forget what the outside world. I feel like I was once part of a rich family, but my family is gone.

We go to a classroom and try to learn math or writing. My mind is not on school. My mind is on Battan and Trivillin. The teacher talks to me, but I just look the other way. She comes to me and asks me if I have a problem. I look the other way and put my head down. I'm bored and depressed. Outside of school, there is nothing to do but clean, all day, every day.

I sleep on a small cot with a thin sheet. The floors are cold inside cold walls. It's a dark, dingy place. Children cry at night wanting to be with their mothers or fathers. I do not have either one any more. I try to stay warm and comfortable, but it's difficult. I keep falling off the cot. I sleep all wrapped up in the small sheet. The sheet is dirty, and who knows how long it's been dirty.

We go to bed at eight. Everybody is in bed by that time. I have nothing to look forward to the next day, just the same as today. I keep hoping that I'll get out today, but I know I'll be here for a long time. Who would come here to look for kids? I have heard that only crazy Americans who want a slave come to these places to look for children, or sometimes farmers come looking for a kid they can use for hard labor.

From time to time, Maria calls a few kids to meet with parents looking for children. I'm in one of the rooms, cleaning. I hear a woman asking to talk to a few kids. I act as if I have not heard anything.

A family comes looking for kids to work on a farm in the capital. I guess I'm not one of them. After a while, I start to believe that this is my destiny. I'm very depressed, wishing someone would come and drag me out of this godforsaken place. At night, I say, in silence, a prayer that Sealie taught us: *Dear Jesus, look upon the dear child. Keep me close; please pity me, dear Jesus. Look at me, dear Jesus. Amen.*

I have no father. I have no mother. I'm on my own. Yet, I'm free. Who wants me? Every day I get up, clean myself up a little bit, and head toward the dining hall to eat with the other kids. We have some kind of oatmeal the government gives us, something that tastes like corn grits.

For lunch, we get soup called *atol*, which made with corn-based balls of dough. It does not taste good. It's usually cold or barely warm. We have a one-hour lunch, and then we wash the dishes and pots. They have to be cleaned really well. If they're not, we get disciplined with a spanking by the head woman. I don't know who the head woman is. I never have to visit her. Some of the other kids who have visited her tell terrifying stories. I do not want to visit her. I'd rather be good.

For dinner, at five in the evening, we're tired from working around the building keeping it clean. We eat rice and beans, with corn or flour tortillas. It is all cold. The food tastes as if it's from the day before—nasty! I eat slowly trying to get it down. I do not want to eat at all. I'm tired of eating rice and beans every day. There is only water to drink. From time to time the government sends other things to drink like pineapple juice. That's a treat!

Every night that comes and goes, I pray. I pray in silence. I don't know if there's a God, but if there is, I hope he hears me. That's my prayer. That he someday He will get me out of this damn, roach-infested, rat-ridden place. I hate this place! Why am I here? What did I do to deserve this? I'd rather be dead.

Anthony comes to visit me once, just to say hello and to see how I'm doing. It's an insult. He is outside; I'm here in this hellhole. It stinks like dead rats. Every night I hear the rats running among us.

He tells me that Dolores is still in Rio Tinto and is having a hard time with the natives. This time a cousin of hers is with her helping her.

"I should be there," I tell him.

I'm in charge of making sure the cockroaches disappear. I have been given the honor of killing them. I walk around looking for them. What a job! Going from a coconut boy to cockroach killer. What a change.

I have lost track of how long I have been here, but I have been here for long time. I don't even know if I have had a birthday. I have seen other families come to celebrate some of the kids' birthdays, but not mine. No one remembers my birthday, and no one remembers me. I have not even seen my sisters, Carmela or Saina. What has happened to them? Are they still alive? Being here is like being in jail. I hope someday someone takes me out of here. Does anyone know that I am in this godforsaken place? If there's a God, why has He put me here? Was I made just to end up here?

I get along with some of the other kids, but at the same time, I do not forget where I came from and what I was before. How I miss playing with my friends the monkeys and the snakes, and Battan, and Trivillin.

Every day I get up to do the same chores over again or lie around bored, with nothing to do. If you don't do your chores, you end up in the hole—no television, no food, and no showers.

I take a shower once every couple of days. I go to bed dirty and sweaty. There's no air-conditioning; there aren't even fans at night. It gets pretty hot and stuffy sometimes. There are no games to play. If I do not have anything to do that day, I do nothing. I guess it's a time to get to know who I really am and what I want to be. From my point of view, my future is pretty bleak. Everything that has happened to me has been my fault. Everything that has ever happened to my family has been my fault.

So what am I good for? I feel like I don't know how to do anything. I believe everything has been blamed on me, all the bad things that happened in Rio Tinto. That is why I've ended up here. What am I going to be good at when I grow up? I know I ended up here because I threatened Lox and Philip. Is that why I'm here? I think so!

I'm walking around one day cleaning the walls, looking for cockroaches. I'm the master at killing cockroaches. I've gotten really good at it. I see these two women pull up in a taxi, and I pay them no mind, but I do notice they look very sophisticated. I say to myself, *What do these white people want in this place?*

They are very well-dressed. No one comes here well-dressed. They either come here looking like farmers or looking like your average person, but never dressed like that. These women look like they're from out of town. One has short blonde hair and the other has dark hair down to her shoulders. One of them, the blonde one, does not seem to know how to speak Spanish, so I guess the other is the interpreter.

I look, and then I turn away as if I do not see them. I'm not about to go near them with my smelly clothes, bare feet, and long hair. I look wild, as if I have just come from the jungles of Rio Tinto. I even smell bad. I have not taken a shower in days. With the hot room at night, I smell foul, believe me.

I pretend that I do not see them, but I'm listening to Maria talk to them. Maria does not speak English, so the other woman is doing the translating. I keep doing my chores nearby, listening. I do not understand what the blond woman is saying in English, only what the translator is saying in Spanish, but she seems very elegant, I think. The blond is looking for child to adopt. From what I gather, they are going to give her a tour of the facilities.

I continue on with what I'm doing, looking for cockroaches to kill, and rats if I find them. Although we have a few cats, they are scared of the rats. The rats are rather big. I'm walking along the long, cold hallway with a roach swatter in my hands, pretending I'm looking for roaches in the cracks of the walls and around corners. I start to pray that Maria will at least consider mentioning me to them. I want to get out of here.

I go outside to do some more chores and I see them walking around. The blonde is smiling. Maria has a scowl on her face. The blonde has glasses on. I get called over by Maria, and I run to her and I sort of bow to her, pretending to be a good boy. All I'm interested in is for someone to find me and take me away from here. I have my head down.

I'm embarrassed, nervous, trembling, the works, to be standing in front of clean people like them. Maria tells me to look up at the ladies who have come from the island of Utila looking for a boy to adopt. I say to myself, *Okay, I can handle that.* However, I say nothing out loud. I hold up my old pair of pants with one hand, I can hardly keep them up. I have no belt. I wipe my nose on my shirt with the other hand. I know it's rude to do that in front of people, but I do it anyway. I'm doing my best to put on a smile, but it's hard, my teeth are rotten. My front teeth are full of cracks. Maria is telling me to smile, and I'm doing my best. I start wiping my dirty face with my saliva I've spit on my hands because I haven't taken a shower in days. Maria tells me to go and wash my face because the two ladies want to see me in the meeting room.

I think to myself, *Oh! They want to see what I look like, to see if I fit their needs, to see if I can be their Latino slave.* I run wash my face and hands, and I rinse my mouth. My teeth start to hurt. I go to the meeting room where they are all sitting. I enter the room quietly. They tell me to sit down. The blonde one is smiling and looking happy. I say to myself, *Maybe she has found her slave boy.*

I sit in the chair, pretending to be calm. They are talking among themselves. The blonde one is smiling, looking at me. I'm not smiling. The blonde one gets up out of her chair, walks toward me and sits down next to me. I say to myself, *This is a good sign.*

She starts talking to me, but I do not understand what she is saying. I try to smile. My teeth are hurting, and they are full of cracks.

Maria smiles, and says to me, "You can talk. Try to say something, answer their questions."

I say, "Yes."

I'm asked how I'm doing and if I like this place. I tell them that I'm fine. Then I tell them, "I do not like being here. I came from a place called Rio Tinto."

The blonde one tries to touch my face, but I'm afraid of her, of all of them, of Maria, too. I do not want to do or say anything that I'm not supposed to say with Maria there.

They ask me if I want a Popsicle. I tell them I would like one. It has been a long time since I've had one.

The translator tells me that the blonde woman has come from the island of Utila. She is here on vacation looking to adopt a boy. She asks if I've ever heard of Utila.

I tell her, "Yes, I have heard of Utila. We used to sell coconuts to Juney, a Utilan."

They are very surprised that I have heard of Utila. I also tell them that I want to go to Utila and work for Juney on his boat.

They ask me is if I have any family here.

I tell them no, I do not have any family. They are all someplace else, and I do not know where.

I try not to be happy. I do not want to get my hopes up too high. They're all looking for slave boys, these white women. The blonde one is not saying much at this time, she is just sitting close to me. I'm trying not to say too much, with my bad breath and bad teeth, and I smell on top of it all.

After a few hours with them, I'm getting tired. I have to ask to be excused, because I need to do my chores and get ready to eat rice and beans, as it's almost dinnertime. I'm hungry. I'm starting to feel nervous. Maria keeps looking at me as if to say, *Get out of here, go do your chores.*

I excuse myself, and as I'm walking out, I trip on my pants and they fall down. How embarrassing! They laugh and I do not think it's funny.

They say they are going to come back again the next afternoon. They have asked Maria for my full name.

They say good-bye, and I wave to them, thinking, *I will never see them again, after stumbling on my own pants.*

I pick up where I left off with my chores when Maria calls me aside. She tells me I was a really good boy and that they are very interested in me. I give her a smile and go to eat my cold rice and beans with the other kids. Everyone is wild and horsing around the dining room. I sit quietly, hoping for the best. I want to get out of here!

I'm not worrying about anyone else in the room, even though I'm sure they want to get out as badly as I do. I feel like a caged animal. I used to be free and I used to do what I wanted to do when I wanted to do it. Picking coconuts was part of my life. I do not belong in a place like this. Put me in the jungle. That is where I belong, not in a place for kids who no one wants.

It's lights out at eight. Everybody is in bed, under the covers. I hate to go to bed at that early. I get under the covers. I wrap myself so I just have my nose exposed. I sweat, but I don't care. I'm afraid of the dark, and the room is pitch black. If I have to go to the bathroom, well, that is another story. When we have to go to the bathroom, we have to ask permission. And, I hate the dark so I don't want to get out of bed if I don't have to. I don't know what I could step on in the dark either—a rat or a roach or I could run into a spirit.

I say the prayers Sealie taught me every night. I'm hoping these women return like they said they would. I beg God that they return. I go to bed thinking that maybe tomorrow, maybe, my life will change for the better. I make a pact with God. If he grants me my wish, I will be good. I start to make plans for my life; I'm going to travel, try to be good, start a new life somewhere else, wherever this lady comes lives.

It's a very noisy night, many of the children cry for their mothers or sob because they are lonely. I try to ignore all of the crying for mama, but it's hard. Some of the kids are causing trouble, getting up out of their beds, throwing tin cans when someone gets up to go to the bathroom. Maria will spank some of them in the morning. She is mean sometimes. I stay still in my cot, not moving a muscle. I'm crying too, but I'm holding in the sound, holding in my tears. I don't want the others to hear. I want my mother too, but I know that I have no mother anymore. All my tears are not going to bring me back to her. All of these kids are crying for their mothers. Why are they here, these lost children? I'm a lost child. I've become part of them. Why? I struggle to understand. Tonight, I can't wait for the next day.

It's another day. I wash my face, but don't brush my teeth. They are so bad that there's nothing to brush, so I just rinse. I comb my hair. I use no deodorant; I have none. I'm excited about today. I have not been this excited that I can remember. I have had nothing to get excited about, until today. I hope this lady comes back like she said she would. I eat my cold rice and beans and clean out the trash cans. I don't have to kill any cockroaches today. I guess they are giving me a break, or they don't want me to smell like cockroaches. I just have to do my regular chores today.

Today is going to be a good day! I wash the windows along the side of the building. It is a hot day, and I feel good. Time is going too slowly though. I keep looking at the sun to see where it is. That's how know the time.

Around eleven, I'm called to the meeting room. I run to wash my face and rinse my mouth. I run to the office, and I'm told to sit. In come the two ladies from yesterday; I'm so excited, I can hardly sit still. This has made my day! I had not seen them or heard them come in.

The lady translating tells me that the blonde lady wants to take me away. I'm frozen. I look at Maria. I don't know what to do or say.

"Really?" I say.

She nods her head, "Yes."

The lady translating asks if I'm afraid of planes.

I say, "I've never been on a plane. I can learn how to go on a plane."

The blonde lady is smiling. She stares at me. She doesn't understand when we speak. I don't know what else to say having never been on a plane, so I ask if it's nice to go on a plane and where we are going.

The translator says, "She wants to take you to Utila."

All I want to do is get out of this place, but I'm acting like a mute, and I don't know why. I freeze not knowing what to say.

The blonde lady asks Maria if I can leave today, this evening, around four.

Maria says, "Yes, he can."

Maria turns to me, "Go and get your things together."

It's the greatest day of my life! I'm finally going to leave this place where I was put to rot, where I have been forgotten by my family. I'm very excited. It's the greatest! I finally have something to get excited about. I don't have to listen to the children cry anymore. I don't know what I did to deserve this! I think all the prayers that I said made it to God. He listened to me when I asked him to take care me. I don't even want to see Dolores anymore. I don't know where she is, probably fighting the Garifuna people for a piece of land.

Maria makes all the arrangements. I have nothing to pack, so I just go to the room where we all sleep and weep with joy.

Finally the time comes for me to walk out of the "bid house." The blonde lady holds my hand. I don't know where I will end up, and I don't care. I just want someone to love me.

It's a sunny day. When I walk out, I know in my heart I do not want to come back. I hope that the rest of these kids have the same luck as I do. I don't know what will happen to them, but someone has found me, and she feels like I will suit her. We'll see. Right now, I'm hungry for real food, tired of rice and beans.

She asks me if I'm hungry. I look at the other lady for translation, and I tell her, "Yes, I'm very hungry."

We get into a taxi and drive to a restaurant. I still look horrible and dirty. They feed me and I eat without stopping, I have no idea how much. I eat and eat, and they watch me eat. I try not to look like such a pig, but I just keep eating. While I'm stuffing food in my face, they tell me that I'm going to go to the island of Utila, and from there to the United States.

I'm so excited and, at the same time nervous. I do not know where the United States is; all I know is that I want to get away from here. It cannot be that bad. It cannot be worse than where I have been.

After we eat, we drive to the translator's house. Here, I take a real shower, a cold shower, I get back into my dirty clothes, and we drive to a department store. She buys me a nice shirt, a pair of pants, and a suitcase the size of a lunch box. That to me is a big suitcase! I'm so excited to hold it in my hands. My suitcase! I don't know what to make of it. I have a shirt inside. It's mine!

Later that day we drive some more. I'm being driven all over. I'm excited. I haven't been anywhere for a long time. I was getting tired of being in one place. We go to take a picture for my passport. When I see the picture, I think I look angry. I look like a killer. I can't believe how mad I look.

She asks me why I'm angry.

I do not understand English. I'm trying to understand, but it's hard. Even though I'm with a translator, I think she's more nervous than me. I'm going to the island of Utila and then to the States. It's an exciting day.

We spend the night at the translator's house. I finally sleep in peace, without any noise or listening to kids fight or cry for their mamas. I'm afraid to put my head on a real pillow. It isn't a grass pillow, it's a feather pillow, and it feels great. I have a private room with electric lights. It has been a long time since I've seen electric lights.

The next morning at ten, we eat a nice breakfast. That lady seems nice. Is she going to be my new mother? My mother! Does anyone know that I'm going away? Does my family care about me or where I end up? I guess not.

After breakfast, we take a taxi and drive to the airport. It will be my first time on a plane, and I wonder what I'm supposed do inside and if we are going to crash. We are waiting for the flight for about an hour. This lady is just looking at me, and I'm looking very frightened. I'm about ready to wet my pants when they call the flight. It's ready to go to the Utila. I'm thinking that there is no way I'm getting on. I'm going to die.

The blonde lady is wearing a scarf wrapped up around her head and then around her neck. I'm wondering if I can have one of those.

We get to the door at the gate, and I'm scared to walk to the plane. I see everyone walking toward the huge plane. It's so high up. I'm scared to get in. I hesitate a bit. Finally I board and I sit down. I'm very quiet, and I do not want to move. They close the doors. I'm thinking, *There's no way out now! Better than spending eternity in an orphanage.* The plane makes its way to the runway, and I'm shaking and biting my fingernails. The plane taxis down the runway and starts to take off.

Chapter 10

Hope

As I board the plane, I'm extremely nervous, taking everything in, not knowing what to do next. It's scary to sit in this giant floating spaceship that I have never seen up close before. I'm trembling; my knees are knocking against each other. The blonde lady next to me is just calm, cool, and collected. I think she's done this before.

I sit next to the window. I'm looking out at the people loading the luggage under the plane. I wonder what is happening—what are they putting under the plane. I reach to grab the brown bag in front of me. The blonde lady has told me to grab it, I think in case I need to be sick. So I reach out and grab it. I'm holding it close, thinking, *This is in case in case I get sick?* I have heard of people getting airsick. I hope I don't have to use it. The plane starts the propeller engines. I stare at the propellers spinning. I ask myself, *What makes them go around so fast?* The plane starts to move to the runway where it gets ready to take off. My legs are still shaking.

What is going to happen when it goes up in the air? Will it fall? I'm holding on tightly, very tightly, to the seat and to the brown bag. As the plane starts to lift off, I am clutching the chair so hard my knuckles are white. I close my eyes and hear my heart pounding out of my chest. I want to scream, I feel like my stomach is going to come out through my mouth. As the plane climbs higher and higher, I open my eyes. Out of the window I see is nothing but land, way down there, and I want to reach out and grab it, but I can't. My legs are still trembling. I grab my legs and hold on to them to calm them down.

I'm hoping that perhaps things are going to be different. I was tired of being abused, tired of going around in circles, tired of not having a real family. I want a family, someone to love me, not abuse me or abandon me. I want a stable life, even if it isn't perfect. I want a sense of security. Even though I do not know where I am going end up, I hope that things are going to be different—a new life, a new beginning, people who care for me. Even though I miss the coconut plantation, I want something different. I am still a young boy. I want someone or someplace where I can feel comfortable and maybe loved. I am tired of not knowing what is going to happen. I want reassurance that when I wake up in the morning, the world is going to be the same.

The server brings me a cola. I am really happy to be drinking a cola. I have only had cola a few times when my father treated us on a Saturday night, which was a big deal to me. I drink the cola, and it feels so good going down.

The blonde lady asks me if I want more. I can't believe there is more. All I want! I'm surprised.

I press my face against the glass and look out of the window, wanting to see if I can see Rio Tinto from up above. I have my face squashed against the window; I do not want to miss, it.

I look at the propellers and listen to the sound they make. It's so sweet! I think of all the times I sat on the beach in Rio Tinto looking into the blue sky to watch these planes go by, wondering if I would ever be inside one.

Now it has become a reality. My life has changed. I wonder about my brothers and sisters, if they miss me. I want to be with them, but I know that I will be too far away. They did not care about me before and here I am wondering about them. They are probably having the time of their lives without me.

I enjoy the sound of the propellers. The clouds seem so close. I want to touch them. I make myself comfortable; I lean my head against the window and close my eyes. I feel so tired. All of this has been overwhelming, to have all of this happen all at once. I keep asking myself, *Why me?* I feel guilty that I am being taken to a different place, but my brother and sisters aren't.

I fall asleep and dream about Rio Tinto . . .

I used to get drunk. I would sneak into these places where they make moonshine. I would wait for a long time until the people left and then come out of the woods, full of ants. I'd grab an old cup and scoop up some moonshine. I would stay there for the longest time, enjoying the moonshine. I would get so drunk I couldn't even feel the mosquitoes,

I was an unhappy child. I was unhappy because I couldn't understand my parents. Living in a jungle, what did I have to look forward to? All I could do was pick coconuts and cut brush with my machete. I was looking at a grim future ahead of me with nothing to look forward to but living in the village, on the plantation, and raising kids with a native woman.

All I saw was darkness, and there was no silver lining. There was nothing in the village that I would say is positive. I was so miserable. All I wanted to do was to run away. I even expressed the thought to my mother once or twice of wanting to run away to have a normal life. She used to tell me, "Go ahead and see how far you will get running away. You'll be running back to me!"

That discouraged me, so I would I go to pick coconuts and try to forget about running away. I used to stand under a coconut tree and looked around at each tree before me. I felt as if the trees were telling me that this was my future. I felt the trees were talking to me so clearly. I was listening to them. I knew each and every one of those trees. I went there every day to pick their coconuts. The trees talked to me. I listened to them as they swayed back and forth in the wind.

I would stand listening in the high grassy areas near the cemetery, a place where I did not like to be. I listened to the tombs of dead villagers, telling me that this was where I belonged, and that I would never leave them. As I was listening to the trees and the tombs speak to me, I saw my future so clearly. I would end my life in the same village where I was *born, where I would always stay, with them. I needed to get used to that, whether I liked it or not.*

I have been angry with myself for being born. I wanted to take revenge on people. When thieves would steal from us, from one of my coconut trees, I would get furious, I wanted to take revenge on them. I had the ability to do whatever I want to do on the plantation without the consent of my parents. They never knew what I was doing. I was free to do harm to anyone who would steal from us. I would think of the most painful, harmful things I could do to them. I wanted them to feel my pain. I wanted them to feel my emotions, my wrath if they came to steal from me. I would think of the most terrible things to do to them to punish them. In the village, there was no law. I was the law. As a property owner, I had to take the law into my own hands to survive, to bring justice to those who stole from us, on my own terms, in my own way, as I saw fit.

I have never seen so many people in one place before. I say to myself, *Where have all these people been? I have never seen so many people?* I think about going to Utila. I'm exited to see Juney again! He wanted to adopt me at one time; maybe he can give me work in his boat. My aunt at one time wanted us to move to the island, but that never came to be; now I have a chance to go to the island and live. I do not know a bit of English, nothing. I wonder how I am going to communicate with people.

When we approach the island, I see nothing but blue water and lots of white coral along the beach and then I see the runway. As the plane makes its final approach, I do not know what is happening. I feel as if I am going to use the brown bag. The plane descends. I keep holding onto the seat, I almost slide off the seat I am so small. The plane jerks from side to side before it comes to a full stop.

Finally, after all that time staring up in the air, I got to fly in a real spaceship—a real plane. When I get off the plane, I cannot stand up. I wobble. I am anxious about to getting off of the plane and meeting people I do not know. The blonde lady gets off and I tag along behind her. All of the people are overwhelming. I wonder how I will communicate with them. I do not know any English or any people on the island. They do not know a bit of Spanish. I think the blonde lady is going to just leave me to try to figure it out.

All of these thoughts are racing through my mind. I am thinking so fast I'm starting to get headache. I wonder if someday I will forget all of this and have a normal life.

I wonder why they called the village Rio Tinto. It means "Tainted River." it also mean "colored" or "painted." The river originates on the Pacific side of Honduras and it runs through almost the middle of the country. It's a long river; it runs through our village into the Atlantic Ocean. The river changes colors from red to green. Only once in a while does it look nice and clean.

The river is red because of all the mud the river brings with it when it rains in the higher elevations. All that mud, red mud that washes down from all the mountains; or maybe it's the green algae that gives the river its name. It brings everything it sweeps in its path to the ocean. We sometimes would see bodies floating in the river, bodies with a machete still embedded.

We get off the plane and I see strange people, English people. They look so sunburned and full of freckles from the sun. They look very different from me. I am shy, and I feel out of place. They are speaking English, greeting each other.

There is a woman waiting for the blonde lady who is called Miss Bonnie. That is what they call her—Miss Bonnie is English. She does not speak Spanish. I am introduced as the blond woman's "future son." I do not understand what they are talking about.

Miss Bonnie comes to me and looks me over. She looks mean, angry, and tough. She has rough skin from the sun on the islands. I feel shy and so out of place. A few of her young sons are there; one of them is named John Glen, the other is Austin, and they are older than me. They just look at me. I do not know how to greet them. I say nothing when the blonde woman introduces me. I feel like a mute. I keep thinking, *What am I doing here with these people?*

I have never seen tall buildings. I'm so used to living in a small village that everything here is so strange. I'm not sure if I can handle having such a different life. I want to see coconut trees. Since I do not see any, I don't know what I am going to do for work when I grow up.

The blonde lady takes me to a shoe store and I try on some shoes. I look at the clothes, such beautiful clothes people are wearing. I cannot believe the clothes that are available. I am so used to walking naked in the village. I want to walk naked in the city also, but the blonde lady tells me that it is not good to walk the city naked.

I take my clothes off a few times because I am so tired of having them on. She finds me naked and takes me in a room and tells me to put my clothes on. I try hard to get used to wearing shoes. They always fall off my feet, they are hot, and they are so uncomfortable. My feet are not used to having anything on them, so one day I take the shoes off and start to walk in the city with no shoes. Everybody looks at me.

I am not used to any of this. I want a machete. I ask the blonde lady if I can have a machete so I can go and pick coconuts. Her friend is there to translate for me. She tells me I am no longer on a coconut plantation. I get sad because I will never see a coconut plantation again. I seem miserable all the time, and I don't know why. I should be really excited about being out of Rio Tinto.

I do not know how to act or to be. I am not used to being around civilized people. I want to hunt, to play with the monkeys, to sit on the beach, to drink moonshine and fight the mosquitoes, the snakes, the wasps, the tarantulas. I miss all of that, but I can't do that anymore.

I feel left out; I do not know what my life is going to be like. I want to live in Rio Tinto and live with a native girl, not in some city, wearing nice clothes.

I want to go back. I miss my jungle; I want to go back where I can be free, with no shoes, no clothes, and my machete. I felt like the king of the jungle with my big machete. I used my machete to cut wood and anything in front of me; no one messed with me. I did not have many friends, because I was always in the jungle, practicing my moves, in case someone would challenge me in a duel . . .

I was training to walk on top of dry brush; especially coconut leaves, without making a sound. When the fronds were very dry, they would make crunching sound when you stepped them. You could hear anything approaching from far away. I practiced walking on dried brush and coconut branches without making any noise so no one could hear me coming, holding my machete in my mouth. Instead of having friends in the village, I would spend my time practicing my moves for different situations.

I was preparing myself in case someone challenged me. I was starting to be good at it, shifting my body weight in different ways. And practicing placing traps around coconut trees. When thieves went to steal, they would get trapped in a ditch with dozens of tarantulas. I was protecting my territory, my plantation. No one had the right to go and steal from us. The land was ours, not theirs, and they had their own. Some of them had about half an acre of coconuts; they had the means to make a living for their families, so I was going to protect my own!

There are few cars on the island. We start walking the three miles to Miss Bonnie's house. We walk for a long time. The blonde lady is greeting everybody along the way, and everybody comes out to their porches and greets the blonde lady as if they know her. I am tagging along, walking, holding my suitcase the size of a lunch box, with only one shirt inside.

It is late in the afternoon, it is hot, and we keep walking. I do not know where we are going. All I know is I am tired, mentally. The ride on the plane was dramatic for me. From the orphanage to a spaceship, a lot of things are happening fast. What do I do with this information? How do I deal with it?

After greeting just about the whole island on the way to Miss Bonnie's house, we pass by a bar called the Bucket of Blood. What a club. It is in the middle of the street, you can't miss it, and everybody seems to know it. We get to Miss Bonnie's house, which is at the top of a hill. Way up there in the back of the house is a baseball field, a huge field, and they play soccer and baseball there on the weekends.

I meet the rest of her family—Henry Bodden, her husband, and her children Bonnie Kay, Philip, Jesse May, and Evelyn the pretty one. She has blonde hair.

I like Jesse May, and she takes a liking at me, I think. She always tries to make me feel part of the family and tries to teach me how to speak English. Not that the other kids don't make me feel comfortable, but Jesse, I like her. She has nice long black hair. She speaks a little Spanish, not much; she takes me under her wing, so to speak, and takes good care of me.

As time goes on, I get to meet other family members. This includes a grandmother and grandpapa—they are the parents of Henry Bodden. They welcome me into their home. They do not understand any Spanish, but they make me feel good. They invite me for dinner and spend time with me, teaching me the basics of English.

There is an uncle, he is disabled. I feel sorry for him. He walks sideways. I never learn his name is, but everybody calls him CayCay. "Hey, CayCay!" I say, and he replies, "How are you, my brother?" He calls me his brother.

On a Saturday night, CayCay goes into town to talk to the girls and drink a beer or two. He's always happy. Sometimes he has his meltdown moments, but he's always doing work in the small corn farm he built, walking barefooted all the time. He goes and does farming just to get some money to buy a cola on Saturday night when we all go out on the town. I will always miss CayCay, a nice man. He too made me feel very welcome in the family.

From time to time I start remembering the times with my family in Rio Tinto when we used to sit on the steps of the house, my mother holding Jacinta, the youngest . . .

Some of us would play under the stairs while the others would enjoy the darkness that the night brought. It used to get so dark at night.

The starry night would light up the village. We would stare at the sky, looking for the satellite. Around nine in the evening, you could see a satellite go by. It would travel by very fast, and then it would get lost among the stars. Sometimes we would see shooting stars too, really big balls of fire in the sky, with flaming tails. It was a beautiful sight to see, especially watching the satellite go by. We had a good idea what was a satellite from listening to Radio Belize. Even though we could not understand English, we had heard that the United States had launched satellites into space.

My father would listen very intently to the news coming from Radio Belize. We heard about all of the big news stories from around the world. My father would be at the kitchen table, hunched in a chair, listening, stroking his eyebrows, smoking King Bee cigarettes. When he was listening to the radio we did not dare go and disturb him. He was engrossed in listening to the news reports. The more intense the news story, the faster he would stroke his eyebrows.

When it comes time for the blonde lady to leave for the States, she leaves me with the Bodden family. All the kids make sure I am taken care of.

I can't say enough about the time that I spend with the Bodden family. They make me forget about my past life; they make me forget my problems; they help me forget about the plantation in Rio Tinto. I am always doing something with them.

Henry takes me crabbing at night with him. We go to the swamps in the middle of the night and look for crabs and come back in the early hours of the morning with two or three huge sacks of crabs—that's about three hundred blue crabs!

We put a huge pot on to boil on the propane stove, grab a dozen crabs, and boil them. We eat blue crab at about five in the morning. That is so much fun for me!

I also go with Henry to take care of some of the cattle that he manages for the Morgan family on one of the biggest cattle ranches on the island. Morgan is a big name on the island. Henry treats me like his own son. He respects me and loves me. I do not know what he is saying when he talks to me, but it doesn't really matter and I get the general idea.

After being on the island for a few months, I am sent to be tutored in English by a nice lady called Miss Jenny Lee. She is an affable single woman living with her bedridden mother. I go to her house to be tutored for about five hours every other day. She helps me a lot by teaching me the basics.

There is also the Hill family, another nice family. Their sons are J. D. and Danny Roy, but J. D. is the most popular kid on the island. Everybody talks about J. D.

Life with the Boddens is, to say the least, wonderful. I feel so comfortable with the family. I feel like I belong with them. They make me feel so good about myself and who I am. Even though I do not speak English, they try hard to make me part of the family. Jesse tries hard to make me very comfortable with them. I like the whole family, but especially Jesse. Bonnie Kay likes me too; she wants us to be a couple. At this time, I am game for anything, I do not know any better. I like Jesse.

I want to settle down in the islands after a while there. I want to see if Juney will give me a job on his shrimp boat as a journeyman.

I want to stay with the Bodden family. I enjoy my time with them. They give me affection and love. They called me their "son." That makes me feel good. I see a family that is not perfect; they have their problems, yet they are willing to fit me into their lives.

Every Saturday night, we all go to town and have a cola at the general store. The Hill family owns the general store. All of us walk in and order colas. I feel so good ordering a cola for myself. We sit at the counter and drink the sodas.

We watch the people walking into the Bucket of Blood, the famous bar on the Cola Mico side of the island. Then we go to a burger joint that is built on the water—actually, it is a huge house with a deck on the water. They have torches along the deck at night and it looks fantastic. We go in and sit down, order burgers, and chat. When I eat, I eat with my fingers, because we never had spoons or forks. I eat fast, stuffing all the food in my mouth all at once. I try not to, but I can't seem to help it. I am embarrassed.

Jesse sits next to me. I feel honored that this Utilan girl would sit next to me even though I do not speak any English. After we eat, we walk around outside the bars, looking for people we know. We are not allowed in the bars. Some of the people say to me, "You're that new fellow who lives with the Boddens, Ernest's grandson."

It is good to know they remember Ernest Lowell. They all welcome me to the island. We go to another place where they have a dance floor. There's no alcohol in this nightclub—it's just for teenagers. We sit around the sides of the room watching people dance. Jesse asks me to dance with her. I am very shy and I don't know what to do. I do not want to dance with her even though I like her. I watch her dance with someone else. I am so stupid!

On the island, they have one SUV. At that time, the SUV had just come out, I guess. All the teenagers are fascinated by this SUV. For twenty cents, we can get a ride. We go to the center of town to take a ride. We all pile into the SUV, lots of kids and teenagers. It is so full; people are sticking their heads out of this SUV to breathe. We ride from one end of the island to the other, up the hill, past the Bodden's house to the baseball field and back to the center of town.

It is so much fun. Every Saturday night we ride in this SUV. There is nothing else to do, and to all the teenagers, it is a favorite pastime. W can only ride in this SUV on Saturday nights. The rest of the week it is in the garage. The owner will not bring it out. That is the main attraction in town for teenagers. When we ride, we do not leave until ten at night. We walk up the hill in the dark, all of us talking loud so we will not be afraid and having fun. The hill is very rough, lots of rocks—big rocks. Climbing the hill, I am barefooted, and I keep stepping on these big rocks. I am in pain.

The next day, Jesse asks me why I wouldn't dance with her. I am too shy and don't speak enough English to tell her, but I think she understands. She gives me a hug, but I am too shy to hug her back, I have never been hugged by a girl before.

She helps me with the homework that Miss Jenny Lee leaves for me to do. Jesse helps me learn English. I start to be able to communicate with people, and I am starting to get used to the new people in my life. I'm not so afraid of them any more.

I stay with the Boddens for six months. During those six months, I have the time of my life. I forget about Rio Tinto, I forget about the plantation, I forget about the time that I spent in the orphanage and all the bad times that I had there, even about my brothers and sisters.

The Bodden children are now my brothers and sisters. They have become my new family. I want to live with them, and they make me feel so good about myself. They make me forget about my real family that I never really had. They take me into their lives, make me part of their everyday, and include me in their family gatherings. Once in a while, the family gets together and has a party. What a great time! I have never felt so cared for and so loved.

I never think about Dolores, never wonder how she is. I totally forget about her. I don't think my mother even remembers me. She never bothers looking for me and I do not hear from her.

Some weekends, when we do not have money to buy a cola, we do not go to town. We stay home and do homework, or sit around on the steps of the house and chat, or play. It is too dark and the terrain is too rough to play outside of the house at night. So we stay in and do homework. Jesse helps me with my work and talks to me using gestures with her hands when I do not understand.

We sit on the porch and we can hear the SUV coming, speeding up the hill by the house to the baseball field, and then down the hill to the center of town. It is so loud, as if it doesn't have a muffler. One night, I position myself along side of the house when I hear it coming, I grab a bucket of water, and when it goes speeding by the house, I throw the water at the SUV.

The next day, I venture into town looking for ice and colas to have with lunch. I hear people complaining that they got wet passing the Boddens' house. They ask if I know anything about it. I say I don't. I tell John Glen and we laugh hysterically. The next weekend comes and we do it again. We wait until it gets dark so they can't see us by the fence at the side of the house next to the road that leads to the baseball field.

After six months, the blonde lady comes back from the States. She has the papers for me to fly to the States with her. When it comes time for me to leave the Boddens. I am inconsolable. I can't stop crying. I do not want to leave them. I am having so much fun with them, being part of them. They are heartbroken also. They were getting used to me being part of the family. Saying good-bye to these people I love, these people who love me for who I am seems impossible, but I have to.

The day comes when I have to say good-bye to them. It is so sad. I get on a plane from Utila to the mainland, Tegus, and from there to the United States of America. I can't believe it—I finally get to go to America. I am going to another world, away from the jungles of Rio Tinto, away from the orphanage, away from the hands of Lox forever . . . and away from Utila.

I am leaving for good to start another life with this blonde lady who found me in an orphanage in the city. This blonde lady—her name is Carmela also—is very elegant. She dresses very nicely, and her clothes are stylish. She seems to have money from the way she dresses and handles herself. I do not care. I am so happy I get to go to the United States of America. I am going to become an American. I am so excited. I cannot wait to see the States, another world that I have only heard about.

We board a huge plane, much bigger than the first one. This time I am not as nervous. This time I am able to talk a bit with Carmela. Even though my English is still bad, I am able to communicate the basics. I enter this huge spaceship, and I sit by the window. I want to see Rio Tinto.

I want to see the place where I used to sit on the beach and watch the planes go by on any given afternoon. I am more relaxed this time. I miss the Bodden family. I hope I get to see Jesse again. I want to ask her to marry me.

When we are ready to take off, my legs are calm this time. No, they are pretty much relaxed, but I am still nervous about going to America. I do not know what I am going to do. I know I am going to have to go to school and get educated, become someone important. I have traveled far from Rio Tinto—to my grandmother's house, to the orphanage, to Utila, and now to the States.

I have heard that the streets are covered with gold in America, that the government gives you money for free and that money grows on trees. I am excited to see that, and to take advantage of it also! This is taught to every one of us as young children. Go to America, get free money, the government will take care you.

Money literally grew on trees when I lived in Rio Tinto—every coconut tree yielded lots of money for the Lowell family! Can that be the case in America? Every coconut tree, every coconut, is money, big money? Every coconut tree is worth about ten thousand dollars a quarter, and nobody has to plant the coconut trees; they grow wild by themselves. I have seen money in the form of coconuts grow on trees, and it's a nice thing to see.

Rio Tinto is a rich village with lots of opportunities, with lots of money, rich in oil, cattle, plantations, fishing, and living; with the beautiful ocean, dark skies at night, sunny weather, and relaxation in the tropics. If you know how to bring all of those things together, you could be rich—but the Lowell family did not seem to have the vision, nor did they see the vast opportunities before them. All of these things were given to them, to live off of and make money from the land, to prosper and perhaps to pass on to the next generation. But they never took the time to think about the future. They lived their lives for the day, the hour, the minute.

I look around; not knowing what is to become of me. Am I going to follow in the footsteps of the Lowell family? Am I going to break the family tradition and start a new life in a different country, with a different lifestyle?

I sit here in this huge plane, going to the United States of America. I know nothing about anything. Maybe in America you need to be smart to get somewhere, maybe they don't just hand you money. I am scared, because I do not know what to expect. I'm not so sure that I will be able to handle all of it. I don't even know how to spell my name or really what is my name because I'm am now someone else's son. When I was asked to sign my passport, I can't remember who I am. I don't even know if I have a birth certificate. When I go to sign my name, I have to stop and think how to write, and what letters I have to use. I am so embarrassed to be around someone who knows more than I do. I look to the blonde lady with a sense of embarrassment for help me. I think that this is the first time I feel illiterate. I don't even know the alphabet, or if my name is in Spanish or English.

I am worried because I don't even know the alphabet, or how to add or multiply, all of the things I should have been learning in school instead of being on the plantation picking coconuts. It is too late to think of these things, about what I should have been doing.

I have all these questions inside my head, but I haven't even started living yet. I'm still young, still a boy. There are so many uncertainties at this point. I have gone through so much in my young life that I don't know where to pick up the pieces, how to start over.

I think there is hope for me. What I do from here on is up to me. There is hope for a kid like me who doesn't even know how he got here—is this the will of God, the God I cursed all the time, the God I hated for brining me into the world? Is this going to be the life I prayed for, or is this some dream that I can't wake up from? Am I going to wake up tomorrow, still living in the village, and then be disappointed?

From the jungles of San Jose to a metropolis in a country of hope, a country of abundant opportunities— am I going to take advantage of the opportunities that lie before me, make something of myself!

I sit on the plane, looking out the window, listening to the propellers. This spaceship is taking me to a new beginning, a new life, a new world, taking me far away from the past, telling me that I'm not going to end up in another orphanage or in another jungle. The propellers are singing the sweet song of hope, telling me that my life is just getting started.

How to Grow a Coconut Palm

Once a coconut falls from the tree, it looks brown. The outer shell is hard. If the coconut lies in one location for a period of six months or so, the water that the coconut has inside begins to dry, and a slimy milky substance begins to take place. It begins to rot, and then a small fruit starts to grow inside, toward the end where the coconut starts to bear the first leaves. The fruit inside looks like an apple and is a light yellow color. The coconut smells rotten, but the fruit inside is not rotten. You can actually eat it, and it has a very soft texture and tastes sweet.

It takes about a year before the coconut begins to take the form of a tree. It has to be in a very humid location, near the salty waters of the Atlantic. Or if you want to grow your own, take a whole coconut with the outer shell still on, dig a hole, pour lots of rock salt or lots of table salt into the hole, put the coconut inside the hole, and allow the coconut to stick out of the hole, one to two inches. Cover the coconut with dirt, sprinkle a little water on top, and let it grow.

Basic Garifuna Language

How are you?.................................Ida biangi
I'm fine..Magadietina
Thank you.....................................Seremein
What is your name?.......................Ka biri
What day is today?........................Ka weyu uguyen
One..Aban
Two..Biama
Three..Ürüwa
Four..Gadürü
Five..Seingü
Man..Yeri
Woman...Hinyanru
Friend...Umada
Mother...Uguchuru
Father...Uguchili
House...Tuban
Dog...Aunli
Cat..Mesu
Sky...Ubehu
Sun...Weyu
Moon..Hati

Star	Waruguma
Water	Duna
Ocean	Barana
Earth	Muya
Baja Mar	Bahama
Rio Tinto	Intintu

For speaking engagements, or other related inquiries, please contact:

sealiewest@gmail.com

Contributing editing:
Michelle McFann
MLMCFANN@AOL.COM

Illustration credit:
ILLUSTRATION PROVIDED BY
Thomas Lytle, Philadelphia Pa."

Edwards Brothers Malloy
Oxnard, CA USA
November 7, 2013